VIBRATION
OF THE
HUMMINGBIRD

TOME 5: THE ASCENSION PORTALS

Illustrations and story by

c. huilo c.

A Jaguar Moon Press Book

all type and design by
Deep Woods Productions
All illustrations and story by c. huilo c.
Photographs by c. huilo c.
For more info visit:
www.jaguarmoonpress.com
www.jaguarlunart.com
www.deep-woods-art.com

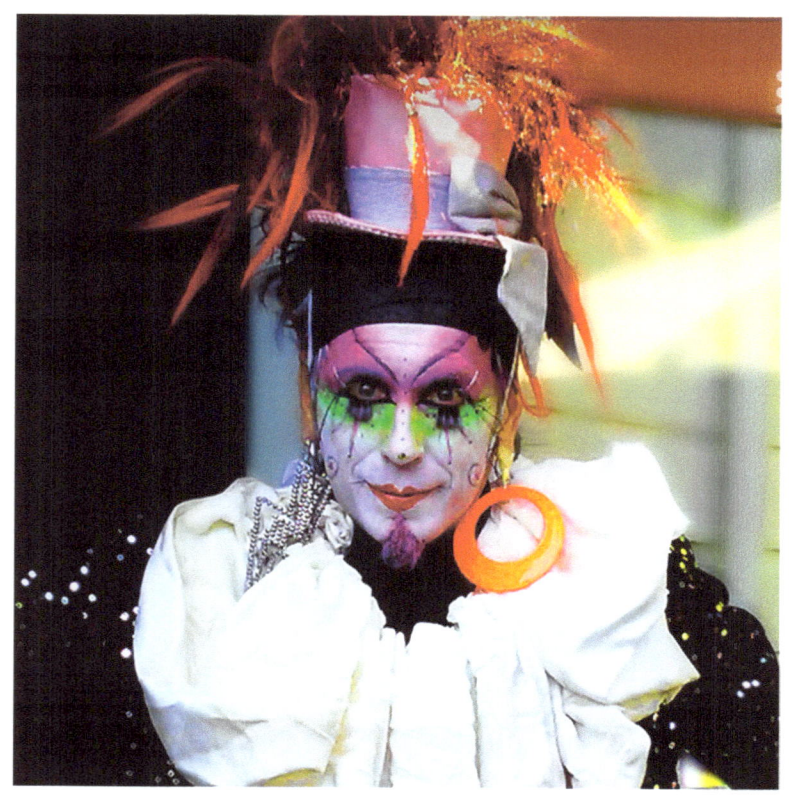

ISBN: 9780985487874
Library of Congress Control Number: 2018942748
Visit www.jaguarlunart.com and www.jaguarmoonpress.com to order additional copies.

 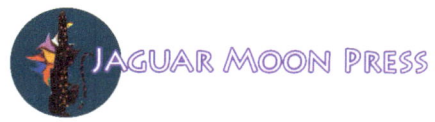

TOME 5

THE ASCENSION PORTALS

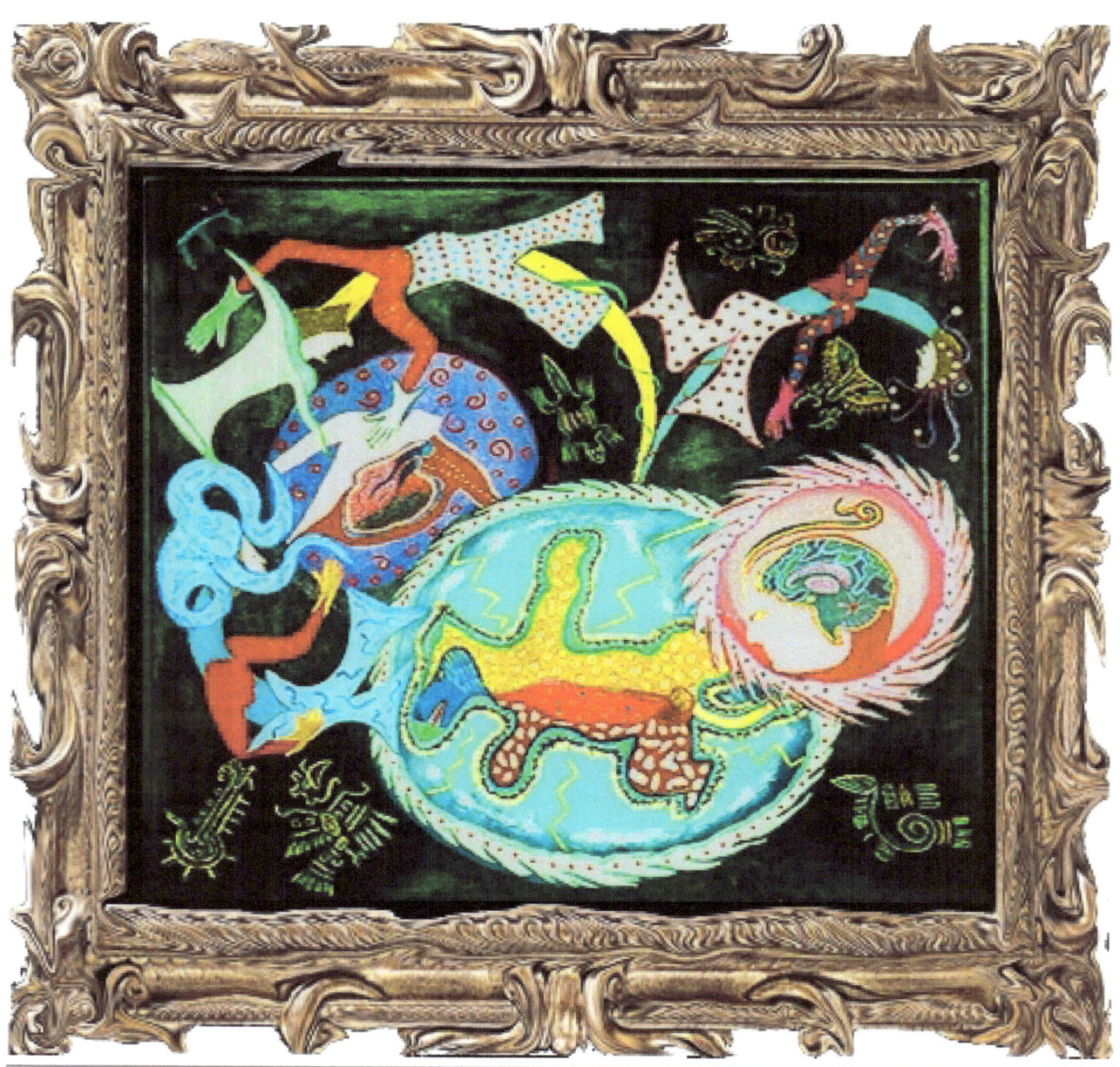

FORWARD

Now, with Lola's accelerated experience acquired during heshe's passage through 3-D world, the jaguar magician prepares to animate the ascension portals for entry to 5-D realms. The challenges and ecstatic reunions on the Planet of Great Consciousness had laid bare Lola to the whimsy of what it takes to transcend 3-D. Moreover, while Lola had gained a direct relationship with other queer beings on the blue planeta, heshe had also galvanized and liberated allies to be ready for moving onward into the 5-D realm of one love and unified consciousness.

While Lola had received the heart keys that would help reveal the gates of consciousness, there were still a few tasks at hand to prepare the final leg of heshe's adventurers quest. The theatre had become paramount as a tool for gathering allies together and to raise vibrational levels. Transcendence of the various attachments to masks had helped Lola to understand the fixed state on 3-D and the nature of identity. Yet, Lola must still discover more, especially regarding the mutability and illusion of time. In order to be ever present of the constraints placed on 3-D Lola must learn how to help humanos raise their vibrational capacity of a focused critical mass attention directed towards 5-D consciousness.

Although the magician had been exposed to various possibilities within the magic of ah Day eN A, there were still vital components that needed to be understood. Lola is about to encounter the magic of the infamous Keepers of the Storybundles and collaborate with the Cloud Beings.

Soon it would be the time of absolute revelation. Along with Ocelotl and others Lola prepares to pass through 13 portals. As heshe's journeys through each of the stunning gates, the quickening within Gaia's realm simultaneously increases 10-fold.

Indeed, in Vibration of the Hummingbird, the fifth and final act in Tales of a Jaguar Magician, we learn what happens after 'happily ever after'. How will the depth of magic acquired and activated in the jaguar magicians be utilized in the final defining moments for emancipation of all humanos from their dependence and fixation on the limitations of 3-D realm? Its time the inhabitants of the Planet of Great Consciousness consider the expansion of awareness to one that is open to everything is possible in the cosmos?

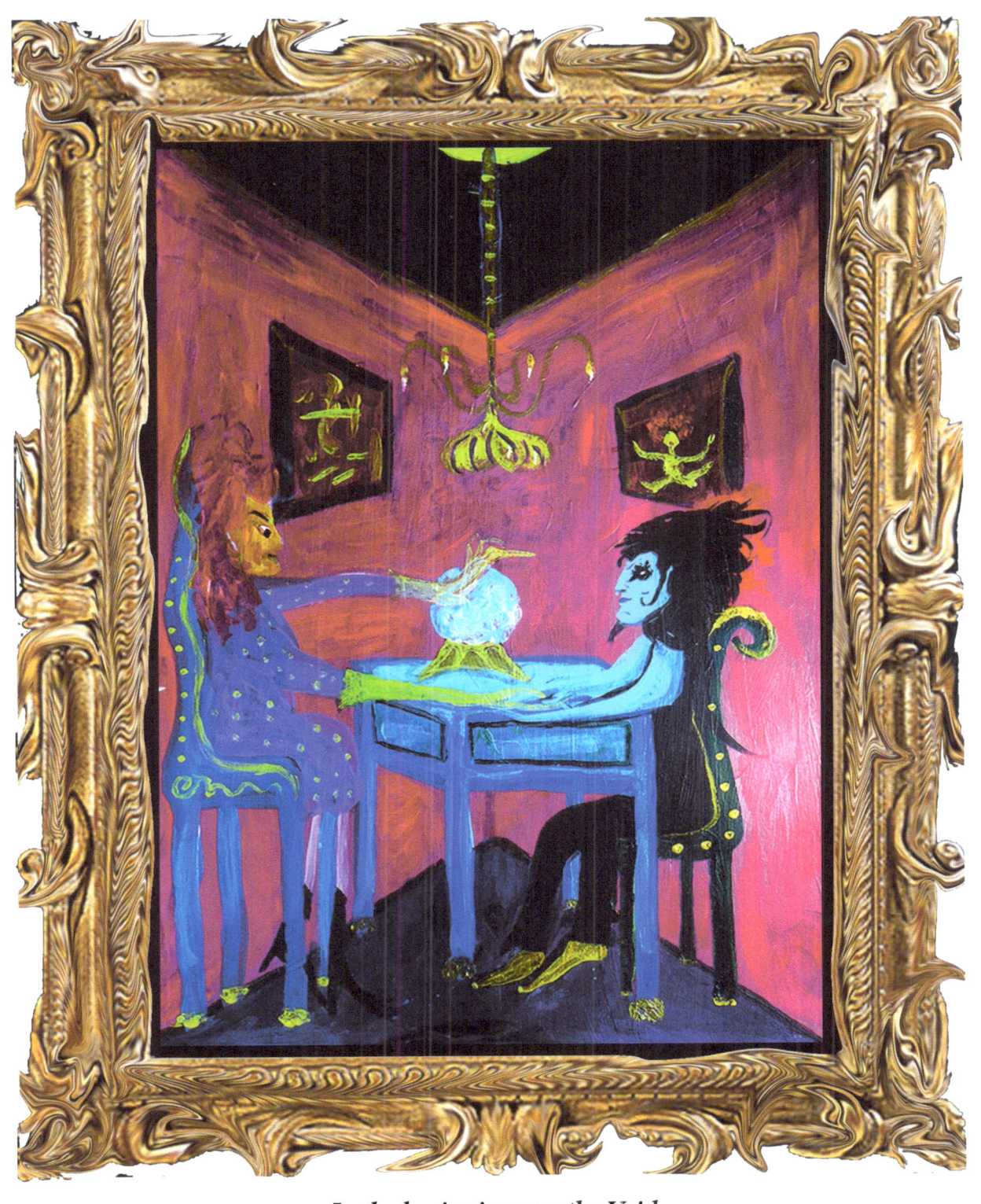

In the beginning was the Void
and within the Void spoke the Word
and from the Word formed the light
and from the Light came
All Creation of the Higher and Lower Heavens

Once Lola stepped through the portal of transformation heshe arrived inside an elegantly decorated room. Heshe was rejoined with an old friend, Loquatia, Mistriss of Misteries. The sorceress sat at a blue marble table. In the center of the table was a large crystal ball.

"How are you doing dear Lola," asked Loquatia?

She explained to Lola, that they had been intercepted by the central guardianos to her 'pink parlor'. Loquatia shared that they were going to review and activate the occult wisdom surrounding the ascension gates. This would be the final step to activate the jaguar magicians. Through this process they would be sealed into being with broader awakened inner truth.

Loquatia went on to describe that on the planeta there was a strong desire within many humanos to reconcile their sole reliance upon solely the techo or natural sciences, and instead live with a more mystical view. This would help restore humanos into a position of centrality and dignity in the universe. With this integration, it aligned them to their innate ability for a more wisdom-centric contribution in the process of soul conscious creation within the universe. Hence, a more focused, direct, and intentional willingness to unify consciousness and live in greater harmony with the 'source divino' energia would begin to enshroud the planeta.

"I have traveled through, as you may suspect, so many worlds since the selva," said Lola. "Yet, I have been taught that they are all one existence and in essence they are a dream or holosphere. Now, I have seen what the humano's world is like and understand more about their quandary.   It feels like their desire to 'wake-up' is a very strong desire in some, while in others it lies dormant or embattled. I can see that their 'effect on the realm of Gaia's is very disorganized and at times violently disruptive. The immense desire to control and to own and hoard material things is killing them inside and out. Entitlement has become viral. There is a dangerous addiction to delusion rather than concentrating and encouraging compassionate illusions or dreams. That said, my good friend, have you any advice? It's clear the time has come. The gates must be opened."

Loquatia took Lola's left hand and then with her other hand caressed the crystal sphere. It began to change colors on the inside and resembled smoke. The vapors slowly disappeared and images appeared.

"Ah, their they are, the codigos de ascensia. Hmm… Yes. Yes. Look at them. Here are the matrix re-codifiers for humanos. Passage through these gates will resolve dual consciousness and prepare them for what's next. It will magnetize energy to expand limitations—and most importantly, the vibration of their minds. When these codigos are activated and amplified, it will build a bridge for interconnectedness and transpersonal relationships with all things. Unfortunately, it was something they had forgotten perhaps from all the distractions and blazing battles on the planeta for millenia."

"Yes! I can see them too! So, what can I do to help," asked Lola?

"Just like they appear to you here in this crystal sphere, they will be visible again on parts of your remaining journey. Now, carefully remember their teachings and realizations. Learn to focus your willpower upon them to open the gates. Then, you can mirror these teachings to others who are ready. You can help those who are challenged to embrace the oneness and be liberated from their strife. First, there will be the process of integration. Placing the activation of the intentions at each gate will awaken the existence of its magic to all humanos. This can lead to crucial breakthrough from the massive density of 3-D and benefit completion of the journey into 5-D realms. This is what you are most familiar with, as we already reside in that essence of **oneness**. Lola, I know It has been confusing for you about why we asked you to go to this realm. Know that all life is in favor, and desires this transition. The Planet of Great Consciousness has a wide echo in the universe."

Loquatia got up from her chair and put on a long velvet, indigo cloak. "Join me with the masters of time. They are allies whom I don't believe you've seen in a long time. Dear Gaia awaits us with the fascinating and mysterious lord, Fabuloso Fibonacciriqweenie."

She motioned Lola to the doorway. "Did you notice how humanos respond and integrate to time as if it were limiting or finite? In 3-D they operate amid strict constraints with physical limits thus a mode that accelerates deterioration after time passes. The physical mass, that is, the illusion of congealed energy, is cumbersome for humanos. If they are to evolve, to awaken as you would like, their relationship with time and space must change."

*G*aia stood elegantly in front of a large device, which looked somewhat like a clock. "Dear, dear Lola! It's been some time since we joined together in the physical realm. First of all, thank you *so* much for all your compassionate enthusiasm that you have shared for our Planet of Great Consciousness. As you've come to know the people well and the predicaments they face, I thought it was important to share my friend's story. As the matrix shifts on the planeta, the coordination of time must also shift. As intervals of time rule a flow of beingness, and we are integrating what is known as the Beloved Mother Arc. This rhythm follows the waxing's and wannings of dear Luna."

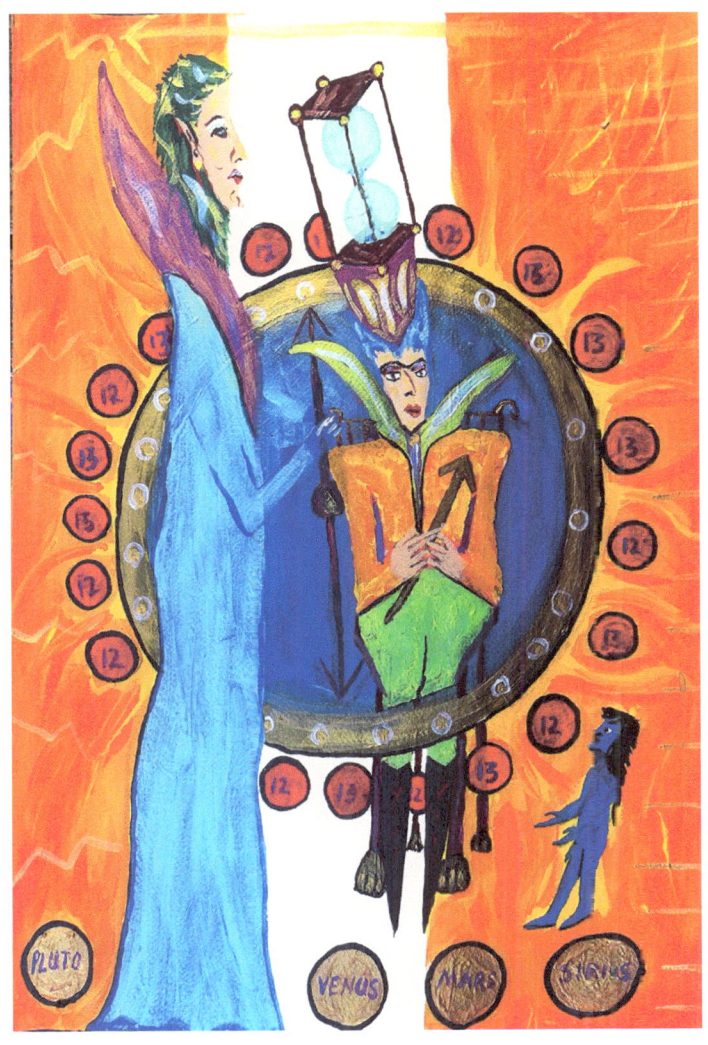

Fabuloso Fibanacciniqweenie nodded to his guests. The wizard gazed around the whacky room that was filled with a myriad of time-keeping devices. Fabuloso muttered to himself, sputtering juxtaposed phrases. "If it's 3 o'clock here, what time is it there? I haven't got any more time! I've got all the time in the world! Time keeps on slipping into the future. What is the difference between bad timing and good timing?

Indeed. What time is it on Pluto? Or Venus? Or on the Pleiades? What if you have an appointment on Mars at five, would you be late if you came from Jupitera at 6? Oh, my and if you had an appointment in the Urban Jungle at the same time, at any time? What time would it be? Can you answer that, young magician?" Fibanacciniqweenie looked perplexed. His brow wrinkled from the weight of a large hour-glass which sat upon his head.

"Ah, yes, I remember the timelessness of the jungle. It was so beautiful. The Sol would rise and night would gently follow, yet, there was no rush of doingness which plagues many of the humanos. I see so many numbers posted about in their world. I saw a reference to the number 108… what it that? And the sequences of 12:12 and 13:13 and 7777 make a pathway to heaven!"

Fibby (as his friends referred to him), pierced arrows and moved numbers around inside a circle where the wizard was seated. There was the constant sound of ticking, hissing, popping, winding and cranking. It was like a strange electronic song, perhaps an ode' to time.

"Ahahaha… the numbers, the letters, the glyphs they use to relate, to describe, to communicate, to postulate. The 1.0.8. is one of the sequences attributed to the holy or 'source'. Now, *why* is that? Ah, well," sighed Fibby. "See this upon my head? It was once used to tell or refer to time passing. Thousands of grains of sand were moved from one sphere to the another by which they *thought* could determine a whole series of events and outcomes. Powerful stuff, the illusion of time. They also built cute little castles on the beach out of sand, perhaps it was better to use for that purpose than counting grain by grain towards an illusory future. One must consider that realizing the *ancient* future is important as well."

"Ah, Lola does it sound like he's talking in circles," asked Gaia?

"Spirals. Spiritual. They love to use those terms. I prefer spiral. Spiritual is a conundrum of objectivity and subjectivity and perplexivity… is that even a word?" Fibby seemed confused at how to address his guests. He seemed irritated, like he'd rather be left alone.

"You're quite perceptive, Fibby. Indeed, it seems like there is so much trickery upon the upon plane of humanos. Yet—now there are so many awakening to new levels—and that certainly includes new understandings of time. Exponentially! They refer to it as the great quickening," offered Lola.

"Indeed! Mago! The unfolding spirals of interpretation and navigation coordination in relation to the continued creation of their world stands at the crossroads of divine paradox. They have spent millennia desperate on understanding or interpreting the ALL. Gender. Time. Space. And now? Their vibration is accelerating and many don't know what to do? They fight change. Eventually, everything will collapse upon itself in an inevitable entropic situation, and then the phoenix will rise from the ashes of what was before into a newly discovered age. A new epoch will be spawned from the debris."

Fibby paused and regarded his guests. "Ah, am I rambling? Well, anyway, they call it the age of Aquarius, no? The age of the Mental Universe. Indeed, they have surpassed the age of the guru, the messiah, and the subsequent aspirations of finding a singular or even multiple spiritual leaders to explain it ALL. As if they could go home and sleep better if they understood what cannot inevitably be comprehended."

"I noticed how they compare the this and the that… 12 things may be better than 10, or 13 things may be less than the strength of 1. As I assist and activate the direct links I now have with the planeta… What can you share on the story of aH Day En A," asked Lola?

"Oooo, ok. Lola, let's take a walk… I'll introduce you to another friend Master Genechro Dee N. eA," stated Gaia. They bid farewell to Fibby and walked through yet another doorway.

$\mathcal{G}$aia motioned to Lola to approach the extremely tall being who stood next to a vibrantly colorful tree. "That is the Master of ah Day En A, we refer to this keeper as 'Genechro'. Go ahead, you can ask them about the formulations and unraveling of the codes that are keys to the ascensia gates. I'll be departing on my own way now. My sweet ally, it has been deeply appreciated by all of us, your teachers, guardianos, guides, ancestros and the humanos, for your amazing genius and gallantry in assisting with the new kosmic emergence on the blue planeta. Fare thee well." Gaia disappeared into the ethers.

Lola watched as Genechro unfurled what appeared to be a large scroll. The giant Master gestured for Lola to come closer.

"Good to see you, fellow magian. I have before me the Codes of Ascension, which initiate, stimulate and activate levels of evolushun. In this strand, there are 144 keys. What do you know of DNA, Lola," asked Genechro?

"I remember a time when my friend, Ocelotl along with Tellurusious were positioning specific strands into channels of thought around Gaia. It seemed they were activating possibilities with the hope of encouraging connections to stargates? So, they must have had some sort of ability to connect power? I'm still learning and I hope you will share your wisdom."

"Power may not be the exact word I would use so much as, influences, or perhaps learns. DNA is referred to as a mechanism for adjusting tendencies of how things evolve or change—even one's consciousness. Devoting focus to activation of certain aspects within strands of DNA codes can guide humanos forward into unity consciousness. As they work up the DNA spirals, they can release unresolved karmic bonds and elevate themselves into an exact alignment to Universal Laws." Genechro took hold of a branch from the spiraling, electric neon tree and bent it to form a circle.

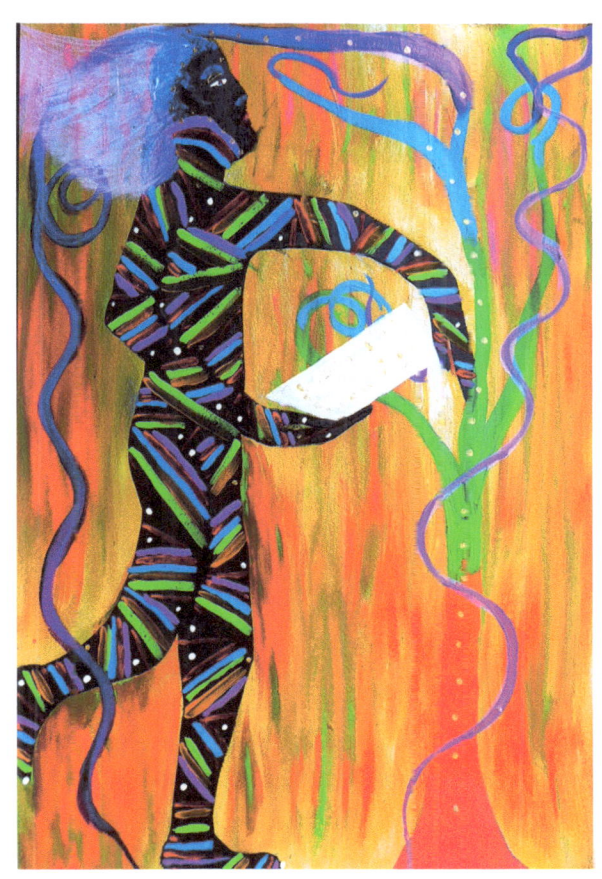

"Some would refer to this as the Platinum body. A location of a higher frequency. After the density of dual consciousness lessons in the 3-D realms, one can invite in a heightened exposure or new awareness of light, thus provoking both magnetic and electric charges to propel them through the stargates of knowledge and into the perpetual motion of the language of light." Genechro laughed. "That's a mouthful even for me! Continuing on, there's an infusion of energy when they activate strands, Lola. Did you witness this on your excursion through 3-D?"

"Yes, I did. My impression is that when they align themselves to gratitude, love, grace and acceptance, they begin to open themselves for reprogramming of the structure for their conscious mind. Thus, this commencement of activation that you refer to in regards to ah Day eN A. I do feel something is occurring at a very deep level, collectively and intuitively. Sometimes there's brutal consequences if they struggle."

"Ah, their insistence on confrontation and fighing! Well then, may I send you on a journey into the region where the Keepers of the Storybundles reside? They will explain better than I about the how the stories encoded in DNA connect. They will also share how the sharing and activation of stories assist humanos with empathy. They also help with consideration for the many other lifeforms, and even lifetimes, that exist in their geneticsphere. This is their story, the journey of consciousness. I'll conclude in that, it is important to cooperate with the messaging of DNA and refrain from changing it abruptly or irreverently. It breaks the universal *Law of Non-Intervention*."

The view was incredible. Rugged green mountains spread across the horizon for as far as one could see. An ornate building was perched on a cliff directly in front of Lola. Heshe approached it and rang a large gong. Out came a petite man dressed in a violet robe carrying a golden bag. Off in the distance, Lola heard voices chattering. Heshe listened a strange mix of sobbing and hysterical laughter. Heshe turned to see a large bronze cloud developing that strangely covered the mountains. The mysts sparkled with tiny golden fires.

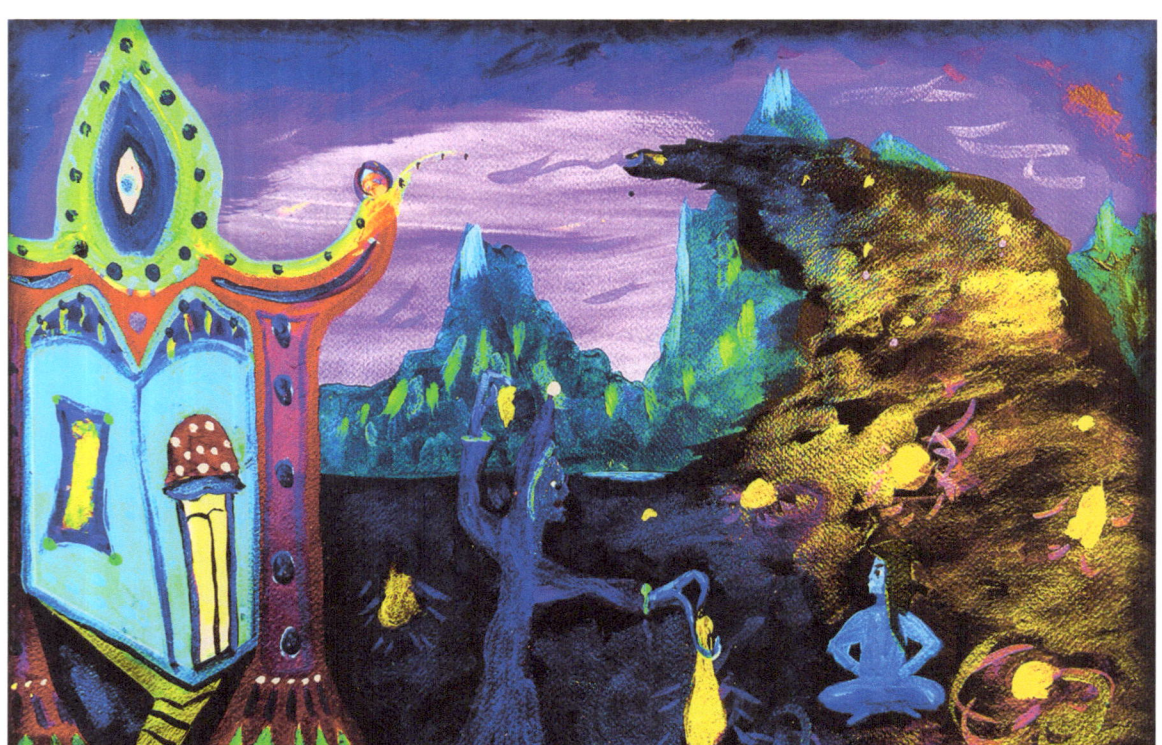

The nimble, peculiar man shook their bag and put his ear to it as if listening for something. "Now *that's* a story!" Suddenly, he noticed Lola and seemed shocked. "Well hello! I am ErMeest. One of the Keepers of the Storybundles. Genechro sent you?"

"Pleased to meet you." Lola observed a building behind ErMeest colorfully light up in turquoise and ruby. It was dazzling to behold. "What a stunning building! If it's no trouble, what can you share with me about how a strand of ah Day eN A carries a story?"

"I'd be delighted! Well, you see…if one looks at each strand of ah Day eN A as if it were a chapter in a book, and as one turns the pages, or strands, the performance unfolds, and the characters deepen their range of possibility. Like a book, the strands may represent volumes or sequences in order to spawn a particular or even collective story. Humanos can move the story forward by turning phases, multiple strands at once, in order to accelerate their development."

ErMeest strolled towards the other Keepers. "Join me? Hmm... Well. Let's see now… there's an old story that shares, if humanos, or any other interstellar beings for that matter, cut or alter the chain of stories they become at risk for de-evolution. Such is the case with humanos and their GMO organism, or even the tales of Dracoids splicing chains to connect and maliciously control beings as slaves. Oh, the tragedy!" ErMeest shuddered. "Well, anyway, why don't you go sit with some of our storytellers and chat with them?"

Lola sat down next to a large basket that was filled with paints and brushes. Lola overheard one of the storytellers speak about how ah Day eN A was similar to painting a canvas. Then, suddenly, out of thin air appeared two of the HairOfants. Simultaneously, a group of humanos started to chant below a huge blank painting. Inspired to join in, Lola raised a paint brush to the fabric and began to sketch faces.

One of the HairOfants stated, "Did you know that your ah Day eN A contains the instructions of how one's face will form? However, the face is also influenced by time, by place, by emotions, by desires. It's true, ah Day eN A can be awakened through focused will and actually evolve during the process of how one appears!"

"Since parts of the face are a portal and represent the dualistic state, I often wonder through adaptation to oneness will future humanos have only one eye," asked Lola?

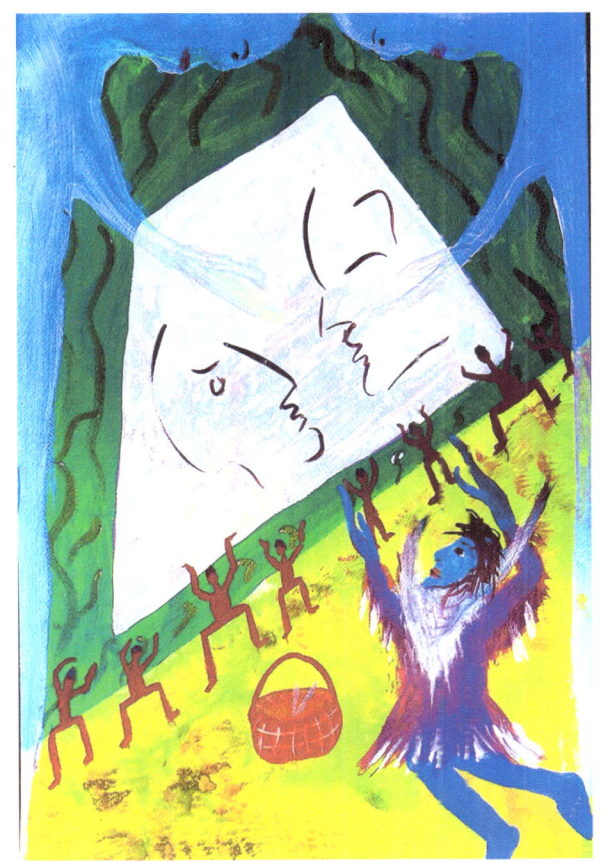

"Perhaps this is already so! In a way, they already do, the 3rd eye. They refer to it as, the All-Seeing-All-Knowing-Eye or the psychic, intuitive eye."

"Hmm… Then I want to imagine them into being and paint the new humanos… as if they are already transformed!"

The HairOfants cheered.   The humanos at the base of the painting began to dance.

"This way, maybe they can see themselves as they will be… or rather… as they *are* when they transcend 3-D." Lola paused as heshe poised the paintbrush. "Perhaps they are transparent… like the wind, yet, moving around space from place to place. Because ah Day eNa A is a continuous story unfolding, is it not?" More cheers from the group.

"I'll paint something symbolic to represent the paths. Something to meditate upon, and to dance with, nourishment, and show them what are direct influences for activation." Lola applied the first brush strokes. "I wonder, is there a way to inform them better through guided imagery? They have so many murals, sculptures, films, and even museums filled with their ancestros interpretations of channels for divine evolushun. If an image stimulated the pineal?" Lola was deep in thought. The HairOfants touched the painting to entice its beauty forward.

Lola continued with their discourse, "It seems to me, that so many on the planeta wish to prevent—or even block their growth. Why is that?"

"Ah… the suppression depression…the oppression of energy. They have created schools of thought that suggest one is better than the other, hence a battle ensues of the hierarchies. If you go my way, you can reach the ALL. When in fact, as you know, by spending time on your own in the selva, if you quite simply focus on lifting consciousness, it becomes self-evident. Remember when you felt alone and Metamor showed up? Alone and loneliness are two different things. How one heals, will amplify into the matrix of the whole, and thus expands unity consciousness."

Lola thought for a moment how reactions to the emotivas, the sensitivity filters could help one to interpret reality. They could also change an experience—even for the long term. Hmmm… Heshe remembered their bewilderment inside the House of Many Selves.

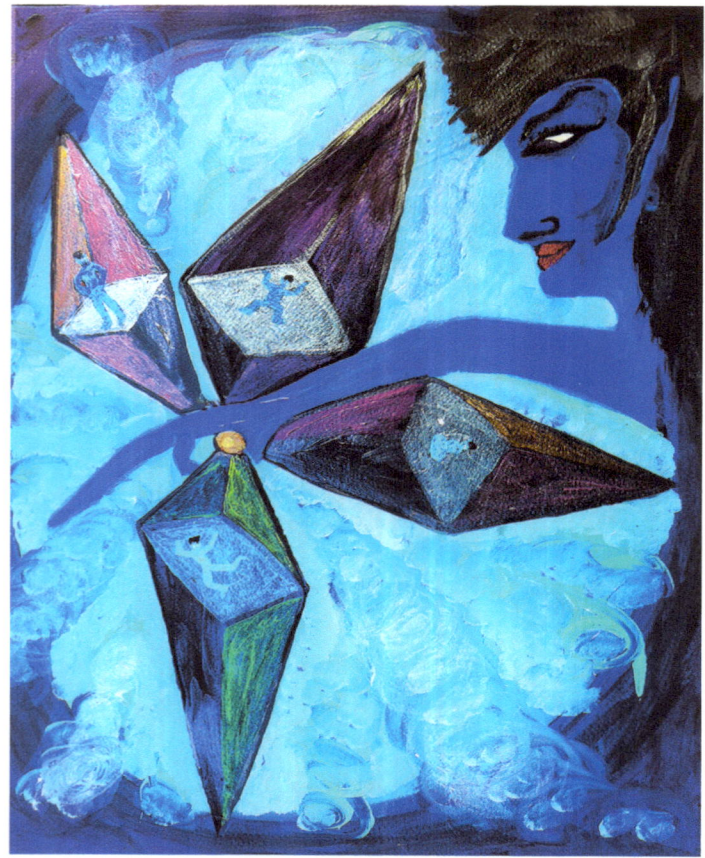

"It used to frighten me somewhat, all the voices in my head. I can't imagine how humanos deal with all their internal voices. There are thousands of ways those voices penetrate and project into their consciousness especially through the myriad of distractions in the techosphere. Constantly, they're self-identifying to someone else's ideas—known as the pendulum mind. Rarely does anyone sit on their own in nature for long periods. A few, but it's not the norm.

You know something, HairOfant? Right now I'm also remembering the magic of octahedrons. Honestly, I think I need to realign myself after spending so much time in 3-D. I want to unify my own thoughts and patterns," stated Lola.

Heshe raised up their hands and spun four octahedrons into the air. They twirled each of them like toys. "I see you in there! Now, with the many Lolas, and myself, I return you to the *I am that I am*!" Promptly, swirls of blue clouds appeared inside the pyramidal forms and joined all of Lola's many selves back into one.

𝓛ola swirled their hands into the air and the octahedrons disappeared. Then, heshe floated up into the sky. This would be the first time Lola was actually *inside* the clouds. Once again, heshe felt light of heart.

"Oh, great stratus beings! So many look upon at you from the planeta and dream with you—or fear your tormentas. What are your ideas on how I can open more possibilities to unify consciousness and liberate the jaguar magicians?"

"Hello, I am Nimbo. This is Seriuuss, Cumulon and Congestus. We are ready to assist as you desire. Yes, of course, we have ideas. No one ever asked." Nimbo lowered itself so that Lola could ride around in the vaporous mass.

"When we gather ourselves together, sometimes we rain. Sometimes we strike energy through our lightening. Sometimes it is liquid and other times we release millions of frozen water crystals as flakes of snow. Often, we color skies so they gasp! At times, we get dark and fierce and send them scurrying. Our only desire is to clean the air."

"Oh yes! Humanos call them Storms. Perhaps with your rains and colors you might add some magica," asked Lola?

"Of course, we are always doing that, yet, some humanos are trying to manipulate us. However, with our friend Arco Iris, I think we can lift their hearts and make some dazzling beauty. Let's compose a symphonic rain and paint the sunset in the shape of a unicorno!"

c. huilo c.   282

"How cool! Cover them with your beauty. I've heard that your water droplets contain elementals that can stimulate joy? Ions or something?"

Congestus rumbled. "Indeed we do, but they live in a fog down there—no pun intended. But, if we all work together, perhaps we can flush out their forgetfulness and replenish them with the waters of life. That should lift their hearts and open the sky of limitlessness possibilities."

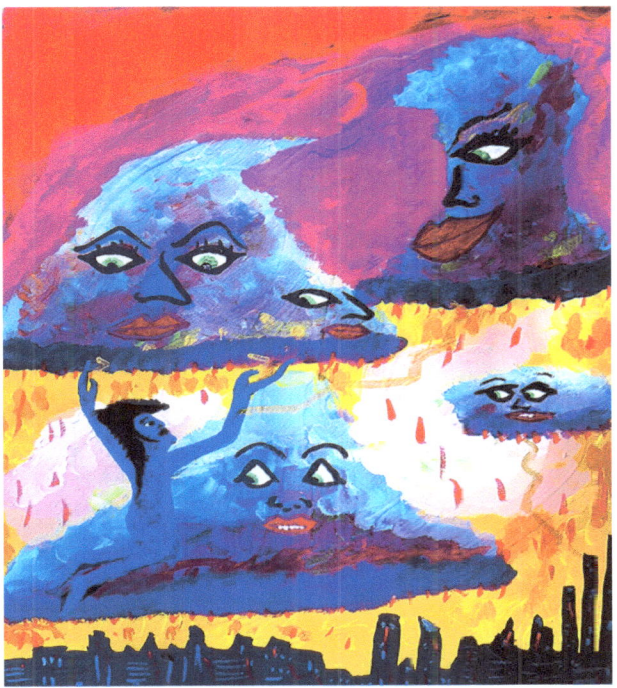

*L*ola enjoyed their visit with the clouds. However, heshe felt it was time to return to 3-D once again and converse with more of the humanos. However, just before doing so, one of the 'Keeper of the Storybundles' ran towards Lola.

"Hello! Who are you? What a dazzling, flaming, outfit," exclaimed Lola!

"Why thank you, I'm in deep gratitude. And, by the way my name's, Rosey! Can I share one last story with you before you go back to that dreadful place? I mean,

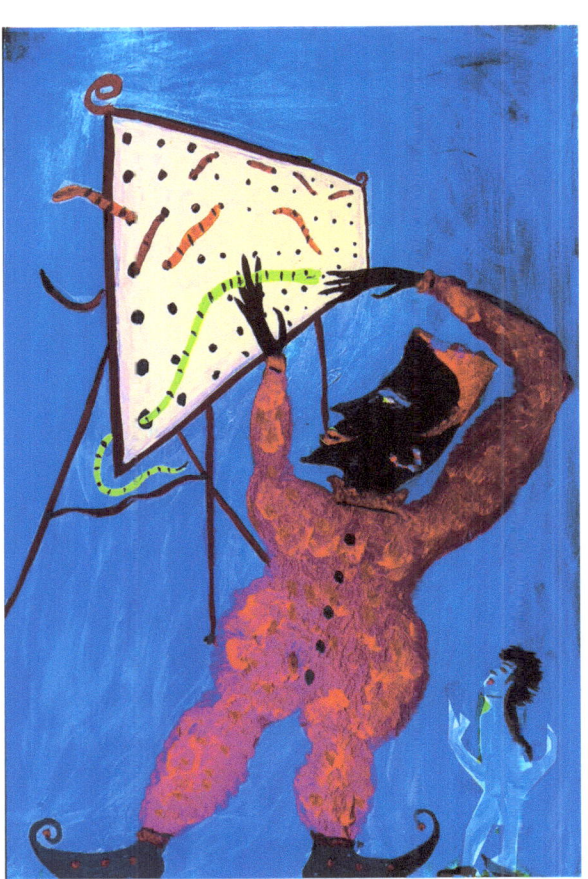

it's not dreadful, it's just uuufff… Honestly, with all the changes going on in 3-D... well, let's just say, the shedding and weaving I personally prefer to do with my amazing hair style!"

Lola stood next to a large easel and observed Rosey. Shw was pulling snakes out of a canvas! "Whoahhh! That is kooky amazing! What are you doing with the serpientes?"

"Why I'm weaving them of course! I'm interlacing a new patterns, a bit like what your friend, Grandmother Aracnia Zuvuyana showed you with her web. But here, I'm illumining the metaforica story of shedding a skin. Humanos must do just that—let go of everything in order to move into 5-D, so, that the body can handle the lighter, higher vibrations.

Pattern tracking is an important skill to have as you continue to merge with 5-D consciousness. Help the humanos know what to look for and cues that they are well on their way. Don't want 'em to get discouraged," offered Rosey.

"I will do so. That canvas is amazing," exclaimed Lola.

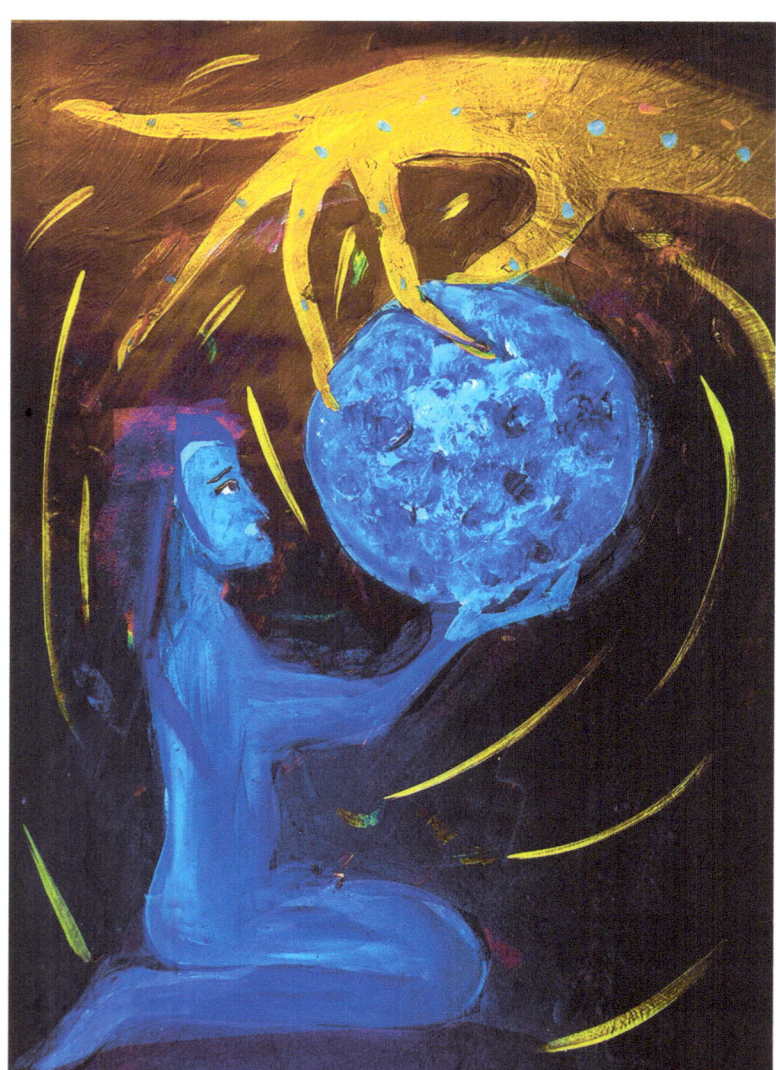

"Thanks, Rosey! I'm on my way now back to the Citay," exclaimed Lola as they wandered off into the horizon.

"Remember my dear, you have the world at your fingertips! Let me help you with an easier return." Rosey took a few snakes and formed them into a giant hand. Then, with the swirl of her magic, Lola was whisked back onto the boulevard.

It was just like that, thought Lola. The world *is* at my fingertips! Everything I thought, dreamed, desired could happen in an instant. Even bothersome realities like shadow energies. Lola gazed at their hands. These fingers had touched many places and dimensions, with these palms up, I gift the world my love, my honor and my integrity.

Lola wondered where to begin. The Citay seemed brighter somehow, and not so daunting. In fact, if felt a bit more interesting and full of intrigue. Humanos did have a way to play with the elementals. Lola flagged a Taxista. "Hello! Do you know where any partay's are?" Lola figured maybe it was time to celebrate with the humanos. Indeed, I would rather rejoice in their transformation than force it or even over-intend it.

The taxista drove Lola to a large park inside the Citay. A huge sign stood at the entrance which read, '*Solstice*'.

"Solstice? Isn't that a celebration of the turning of celestial cycles," asked Lola?

"Not this one… it's the name of a band, with music for danceing" replied the taxista.

"Ah! Then, I will dance with them in their liberation and celebrated the restoration of equilibrium to their star, Sol-fyre. Dancing is a way for them to connect to spirits, why don't come join me, Taxista?"

"You know, I have to work, but, what the heck? I love living in the moment! Spontaneity rocks! Ill join you of course!" And they went into the park arm in arm and danced until the stars came out.

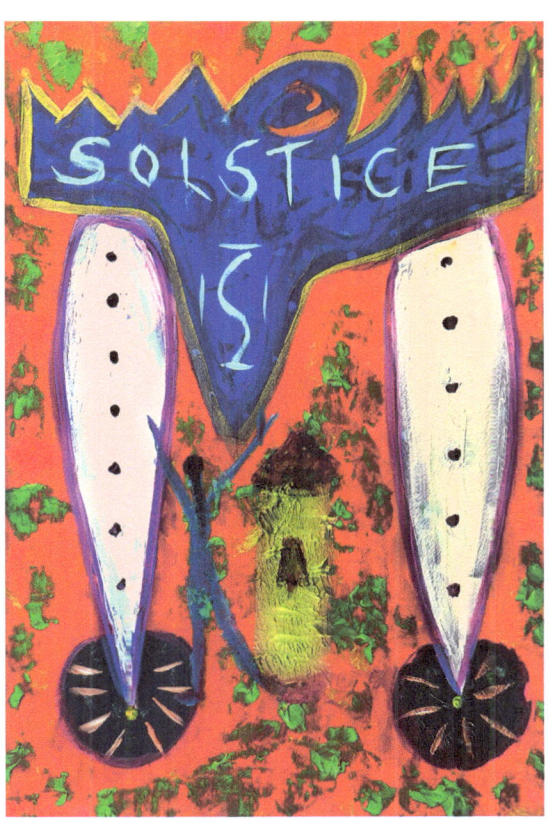

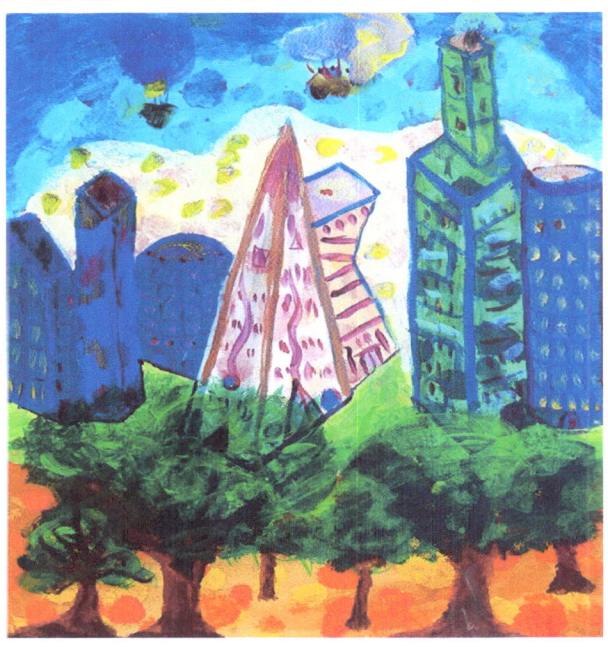

After dancing, Lola strolled through the Metropoli-Citay. As heshe walked along the boulevard they looked up at the sky. It seemed the Cloud beings had kept their promise. The sky looked absolutely magical. Trees had sprouted and bloomed everywhere— even from the tops of skyskrapers. Huge balloons transported people around the sky. The humanos, it seemed, were, at last focusing their will on worthy things. Even the colors of the buildings had changed into vibrant, enchanting illuminations. As Lola passed the structures they felt an electrical burst of joy. Lola began to spin wildly in the streets. In turn, many others joined heshe. Everyone laughed joyfully and filled the hundreds of parks dispersed throughout the city. The potential of conscious evolution was becoming quite apparent.

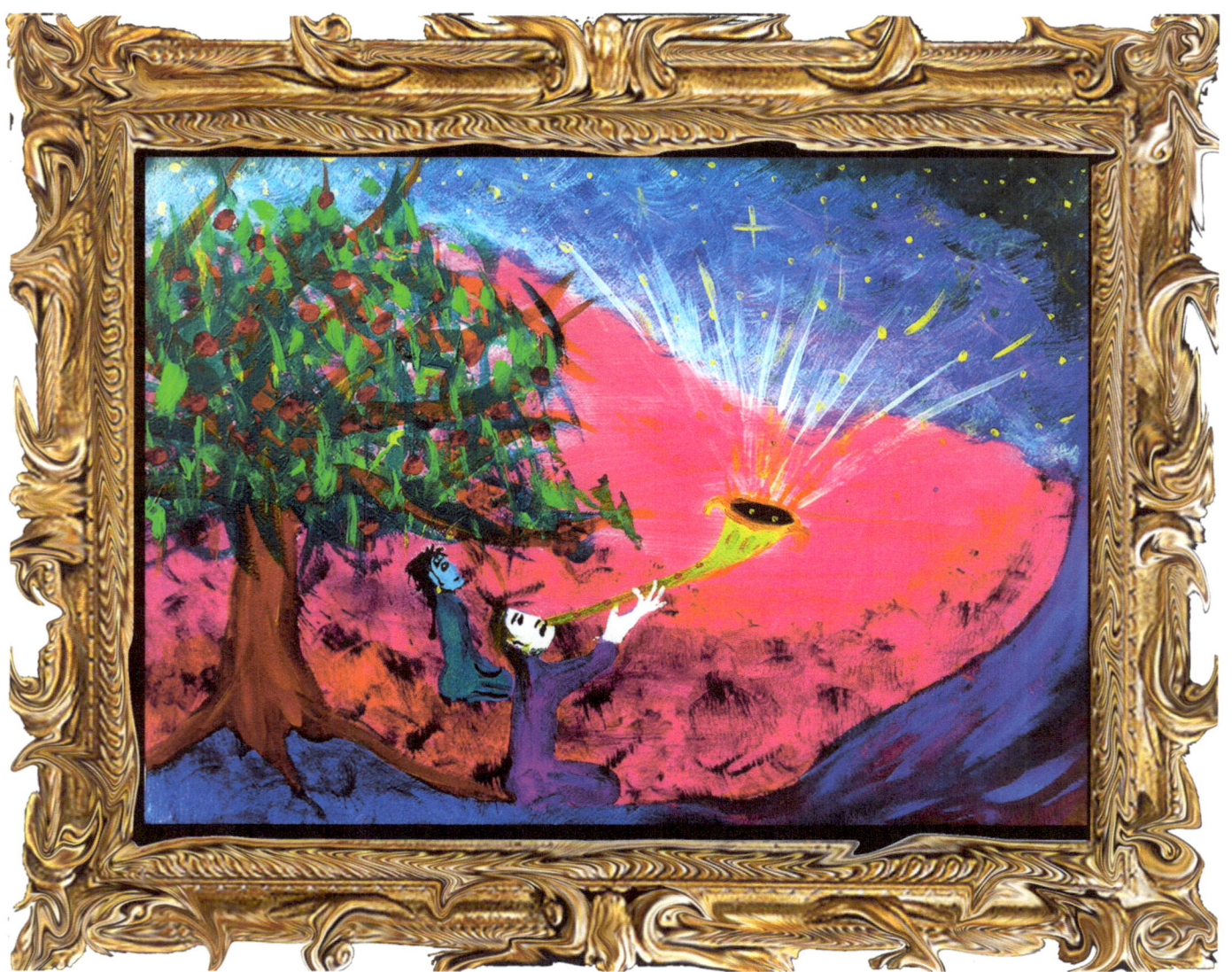

$\mathcal{L}$ola continued strolling until they arrived at a large field, just as dusk arrived. Truly, it was the beginning of a lovely evening. Lola heard music nearby and looked around to locate where it was coming from. Heshe saw a young humano blowing into a long trumpet. Sparks were coming out of the horn and flying into the sky!

"Wow! That's so cool. Is the horn used as a conjuring tool," asked Lola?

The fascinating boy sat down the golden horn and smiled at Lola. "I am Starsinger. I have heard of you. You are Lola. It is so good to have you join me this night. I am practicing singing forth the stars."

"So that is what you're doing?! Honestly, that music could summon anything," swooned Lola. "How did you learn to do this?"

"It's in my ah Day eN A," laughed Starsinger! "I was sitting under this tree a few suns back and noticed a star falling to earth. I walked over and heard the star-being weeping. I got nearer and asked, how could I help ease her pain?"

"What did she say," asked Lola?

"Well, she offered that the vibration of humanos had fallen so low, and that they had befouled the skies so much, that soon they would no longer be able to see the stars. The celestial beings could also not hear them! She was concerned that inhabitants of the Citays were not experiencing the medicine of star beings—even if it was only to behold them with their eyes at night. Their skies were no longer dark enough because all the lights had blocked out the stars. But, most importantly we can no longer see humanos. It was becoming more difficult to converse with them as we had in the past. Star-beings provide important conduits of intelligences on navigation of behaviors and location."

"Oh my! That is horrible! Is there anything I can do to help? I asked the star. I know that some humanos still rely upon course-plotting and pattern tracking of the twinkling stars for guidance. Astrologee." Starsinger couldn't help himself and got emotional. A few tears fell across their face.

"So, she continued on, "Indeed. We need more bringers of the stars. As they are channels for important energy. If humanos broke the chain of stories from the heavens, it would be a dis-aster. Humanos would succumb to ignorance and rely upon vapid control from unruly leaders. Then, she gifted me with this golden horn." Starsinger offered the magical bone to Lola for closer observation.

"She shared with me, that if I played it every night, the stars would hear the vibration of Gaia's realm and would continue to illumine themselves even brighter and with stronger vibrations. This would hopefully help reach those lost in the veil of forgetfulness in the citays."

Lola looked up the heavens. There were millions of stars. Lola remembered the time heshe experienced with Gaia and Nunki. Together, the three healers had gone to observe jaguar magicians in the urban jungle.

"Come now, I want to show you something else the star revealed to me!" Starsinger took Lola's hand and walked deeper into the forest.

"*W*owza! What a gorgeous lake! It's so heavenly blue. Crystal clear!" Lola turned their gaze downward and saw their own reflection in the water. Even the stars' reflections danced on the waves.

"Lola, this lake has the name, Lago de Despierta'. It's said to hold the waters of emergent materialization."

Just then, an enormous face appeared from the heavens. It was deep violet with reddish eyes and blue lips. The being began to blow across the water. Glistening waves began to ripple from the center.

"Who is this that has joined us," asked Lola?

"Lola, it is me, Luna Oscuro. I have come to show you the heritage way. These are the rebirthing waters of the were-jaguars. Let me summon their masterful teacher, Jaguar Xeshbalami."

The moon hummed a low buzzing noise. Then, it abruptly changed into a sharp, piercing whistle. Luna Oscuro roared. Suddenly, from the mysts of the lake appeared a large felina. Lola heard Xeshbalami purring loudly.

Xeshbalami seemed to get larger with each breath. The feline shook water from its spotted amber fur.

"Welcome old friend. This is Lola, one of your kinfolk from the many realms known as the Selva. Heshe is a student of Ocelotl. Would you share the story of transformation sequences for jaguar magicians," asked Luna Oscuro?

The great felina was slow to speak. "hmmmm… mmmmm…. uhmmm…. Mmm…. This lake. This lago. This water. Washes away. Cleanses one of time. Of identity. The depths of which bring forth vision and integrity. It shapes the layers of mastery …of heart-knowing. Living in the moment. Your teacher, Ocelotl knows of these aquatic tranifestations."

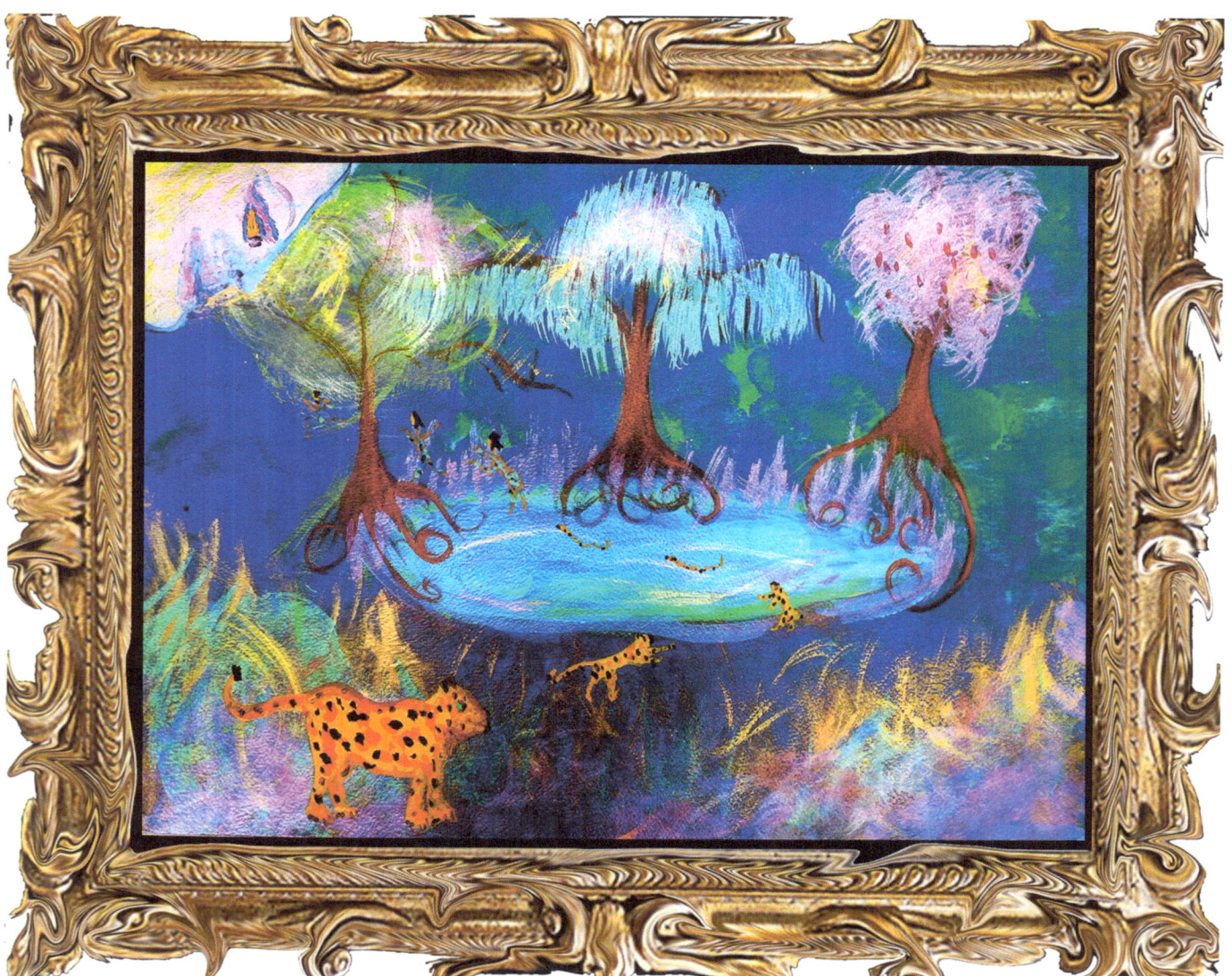

Then, Xeshbalami did something so amazing, it made Lola gasp. The felina entered the lago. While Luna Oscuro blew upon the surface, Starsinger played the golden horn. The magical jaguar swam across the lake. When it reached the center, the large cat submerged itself into the water's depths. For along time there was only silence and not a single ripple on the water. Then, like a phantasma, Xeshbalami emerged on the opposite shore. The felina was changing forms! As it crawled upon the land it began to metamorphosize into a humano with long, black hair!

Lola, kneeled to the ground and took handfuls of water and let them flow over their head. Luna Oscuro motioned for Lola to enter the waters. Heshe did so as well and submerged into the depths of the liquid magic. Below the water's surface, Lola could feel a release of energy, of density and a shifting of heshe's very bones.

When Lola emerged from the water and looked down at their feet it was the reverse of Xeshbalami. Lola's feet were now paws. Heshe looked behind and saw a beautiful spotted tail.

"This is you, your power, your ancestry, your starseed ah Day eN a," declared Luna Oscuro.

Lola took a deep breath and followed the transformed Xeshbalami into the forest.

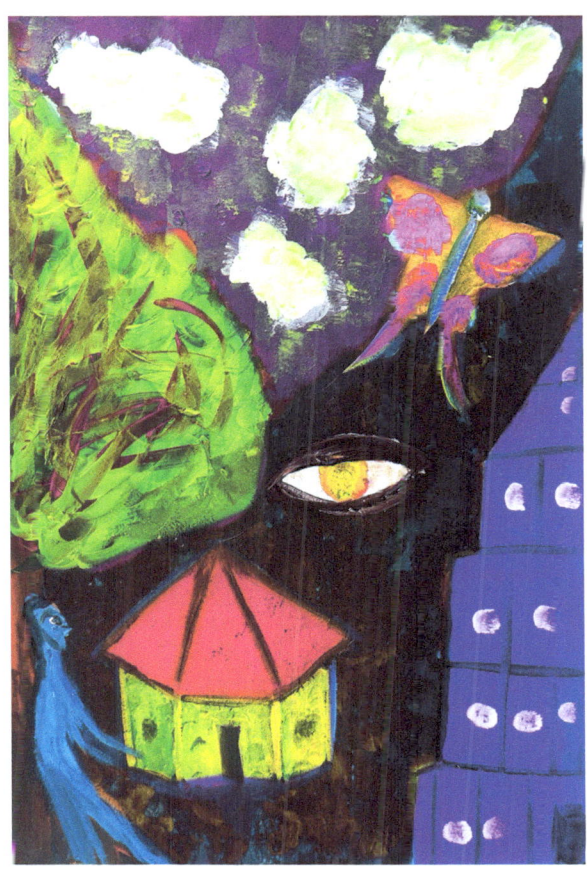

ℬefore they left the magical forest, Xeshbalami showed Lola how to transform the jaguar form and regain the original self-code of humano form. Xeshbalami, explained to Lola it was possible at any time to change at will. Together, they strolled into an open field.

Lola gazed upon it all—the vastness of the Metropoli. There in the distance was the House of Many Possibilities, where Magian Purpol had opened door number seven. The All-Seeing-All-Knowing-Eye also appeared. Then—was it so? Metamor! Lola could not contain heshe's thrill at seeing a dear, old friend from La Selva.

"My, my Hey you… old friend. Shwew, eh?" Metamor fluttered down and landed on the roof of the 8-sided yellow house of possibilities.

"Well? Where to now, Lola?" The butterfly giggled. "Any words of wisdom after your 3-D dimensia swirl?"

"Oh Metamor! Well, first off, the teachings from the ancient future with all of you, Gaia, Ocelotl and the others sure came in handy. I do believe humanos are hearing the messages—many of them. In fact, Xeshbalami at the lake. Wow! Incredible! I feel whole. And of course, the master disappeared fast…like you all do!"

Lola smiled. "I feel recharged somehow, like tingly all over. That lago was amazing for sure. Maybe if we could dump all the humanos in it," laughed Lola? "In any case, whatever is next on my path will surely lead to the mirror of liberation."

"Indeed! What do you consider awakening to mean? Now, that you've surveyed their fixed-world and the infinite wisdom within it," asked Metamor?

Lola thought for a moment. Gazing out upon the sparkling Metropoli and the forests off in the distance. Heshe gazed at the house of possibilities. They fondly remembered Magian Purpol and heshe's subsequent choice of gates.

"ℋonestly Metamor? The story of Ego has been the most intense. Learning more about it from the humano perspective shifted everything for me. I was naïve in the beginning. But what I understand now is I needed to be brought forth from that state, so that the formlessness and innocence of the ALL was completely fresh within my memoria to help others metamorphosize.

I had this desire to find and initiate other double-spirits, some who called themselves Qweers… and I walked about gathering the various medicinas and tools to do so … or at least have them at my side. And then, Ocelotl and Phoenix sent me into the iris of the All Seeing Knowing Eye to grasp the 3d world… to feel it, to know it personally.

Then, I could mirror and reflect my consciousness into their fixed reality. This experience with Xeshbalami illumined that even more so." Lola's eyes widened as if they could now see through, or into anything with a new truth.

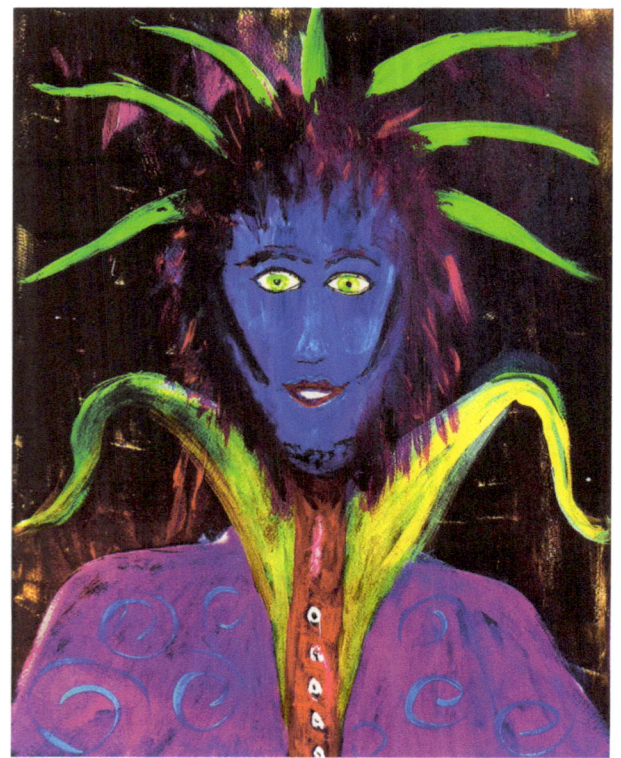

"I do believe humanos can and will evolve. They respond well to imagery and sensation with their knowledge, although with very limited senses. However, I still feel like I may be missing something. These vibrations of the subtle worlds are inherently critical to evolving and lifting up humanos... but how so? I wonder," said Lola.

"Oh Lola, how profundo! Fly with me a minute. Ocelotl and Phoenix wait for you at the recodifier pyramatrix." Metamor flapped their wings.

$\mathcal{L}$ola approached Ocelotl and Phoenix with the calmness of meeting longtime friends. Heshe always enjoyed their time together as it was always uplifting, albeit extremely mysterious. They gathered silently, and after some pleasantries, gathered around an enormous pyramid that emitted bright orange electric sparks. The All-Seeing-All-Knowing-Eye opened up from the sky as Phoenix descended. "Hey there great ally Lola! Welcome to the pyramatrix recodifier," said Ocelotl. "I am delighted you will join us as we activate the theta waves. We invite in this energy to enhance creative expression and compassionate generation for the New Gaia realm of 5-D. The top of the pyramatrix symbolizes and connects to the pineal zone inside humanos cerebrums."

"Wow, how cool. What are all those lines glowing on the pyramatrix," asked Lola?

"These are aligners. They emit codes to directly support opening minds on the planeta." Ocelotl continued. "It kind of gently tranquilizes them to the natural rhythm inside the core of the planeta. This helps relax their anguish and fears. But, rest assured, it is not without free will, as no one can feel it unless they invite them inside. Let's just say these waves are guidance for navigation points of a cosmic consciousness map. These waves are like vitamins that nourish the spectrum of synchronicities within the holographica. They create vivid pictures that escort them into 5-d phenomena."

The pyramatrix vibrated and pulsed as it spread waves out from the center.

The All-Seeing-All-Knowing-Eye declared, "What the dual mind associates with problems... this gives ego attachments a moment to rest. It is a moment to pause and make sense of things. The velocity of change during a consciousness dimensional recalibration are swift and accurate. We are offering a moment of...how shall we say, "*super learning*"?

The group meditated for a while. Lola continued to sit in front of the pyramatrix and absorb its magica, while focusing an intention of clarity.

After some time, Lola stood up and stretched. Ocelotl joined heshe and pointed to the Citay.

"Now, Lola, my friend, I invite you to go back to 3-d once more. Some of the jaguar magicians will be waiting for you, only this time they, too, will be liberated. Fly with them and bring them to our dimension." Ocelotl waved goodbye to his friend.

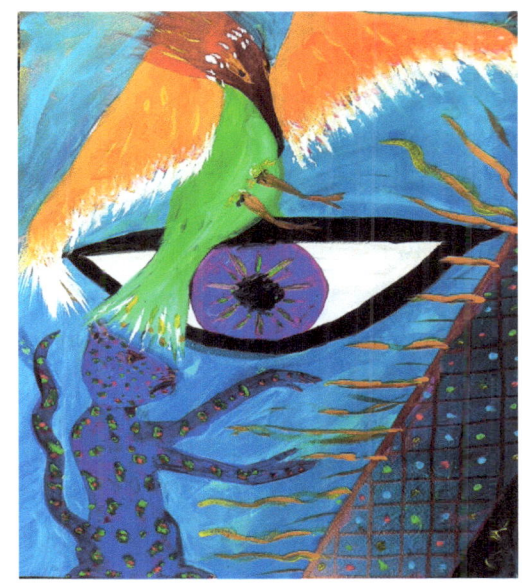

Lola sauntered for a bit through a large grass field. Heshe glimpsed the For-Get-Me-Knots who waved at Lola from the forest. A large group of humanos promenaded towards the Citay. It looked as if they had just come from the direction of the Theatre of the Moon Jaguar. Many of them were humming and smiling.

"Hey, you're Lola aren't you," inquired one of the pilgrims?

"Why yes, I am! How was the show," asked Lola?

"By the way, I'm known as, Jaguarella. And, as for the show, it was quite revealing! I think it roused more of us into an initiated state." Jaguarella paused and tilted their head. "Listen can you hear them? That humming sound, it's theta waves. It makes me feel like I could fly!"

Lola took Jaguarella's hand and wandered for a bit vibrating along with the others.

Come fly with me!

High into the sky!

Lift our souls!

Fill our bowls!

With glee!

As we flee!

This world

In a twirl!

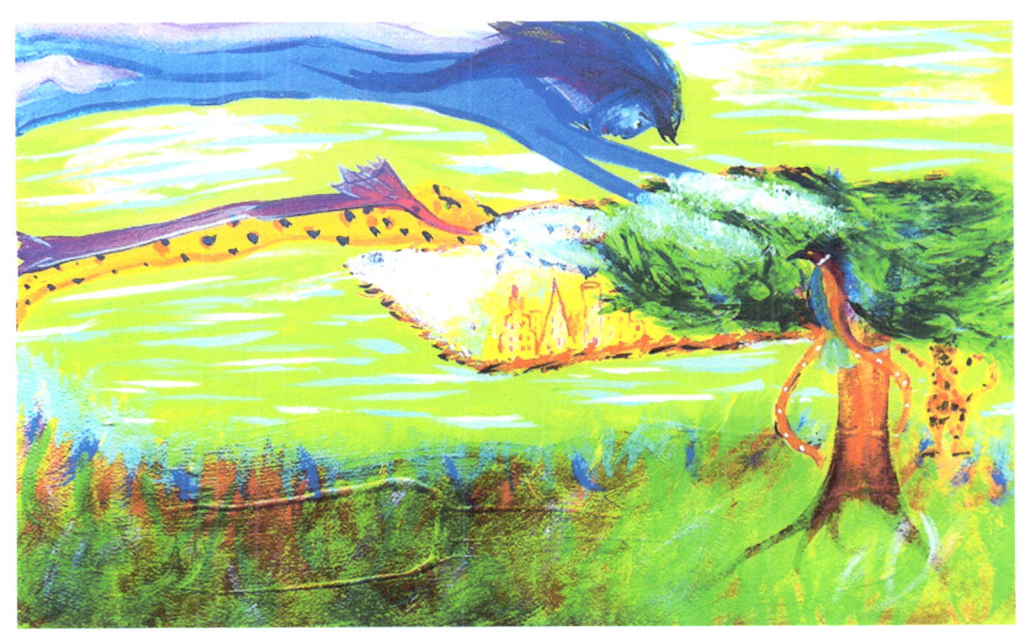

Together, along with Jaguarella, they lifted their spirits into the air and flew towards Arbol de Vida and Ocelotl who were waiting for them on the horizon.

"See, your super powers have come back… Jaguarella! Jejejee. You can fly," laughed Lola!

"Wow, cool! Of course, I can!" Jaguarella soared through the clouds by Lola. "Where are we headed?"

"I want you to meet my friends. They are my teachers, Ocelotl and Phoenix."

Off in the distance there was an opening in the skyline. In the hole, they could see a Metropoli, though vastly different from the old urban jungle. These towers seemed to radiate and emanate a sort of peacefulness.

Lola left Jaguarella to soar into the new Metropoli on their own. Heshe joined Ocelotl and Phoenix under the Arbol de Vida. Lola looked back and watched as Jaguarella lured others to fly with them into the spiraling vortex that lead to the Citay.

"That portal is referred to as the Emerald Gate." Ocelotl motioned to the vaporous hole. "Well, Lola, we have arrived to the time for opening the ascensia gates. They are like stairs. Each one offers an opening

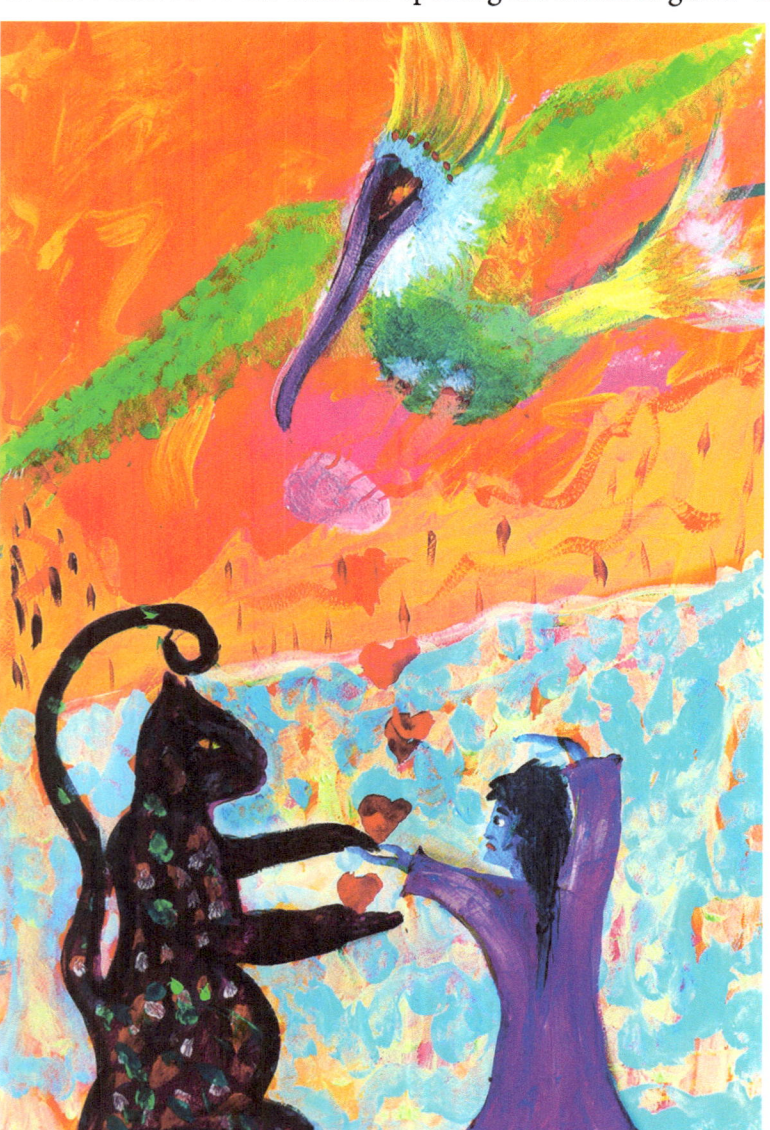

and activation to the humanos ah Day eN A matrix. For now, there are thirteen of them. They ultimately bring forward the vibration of the flower kissers… or to them known as the 'hummingbird'. This is a critical mass of vibratory level needed to transcend the density and elevate to light formation.

Did you notice that many humanos were humming like birds after they left the Theatre of the Moon Jaguar?"

"In fact, I did." Lola paused. "I intend to ascend these steps with each of them inside my heart. Therefore I shall come to know what the humanos will experience." Lola was ready. Their entire life, mission, quest had been for this moment. Finally it was time to awaken the qweer, double-spirit, jaguar magicians and their allies to the oneness of 5-D. The gifts of what Lola had experienced in La Selva would be eveyone's to enjoy.

Phoenix flapped their immense wings. "Of course. Lola. Now, from my Kosmic Ourubus Egg arrive the keys. These heart-shaped roses are magical. In this central pump of life force through their corazones, flows liquid light, or the sangre de vida. The keys are a metaphor for that energy.?

"This, Lola, is heart-knowing. It will invite anyone passing into 5-D realm to finally let go and end their egotistical battles. To enjoy the passions of life. This is a new world that

c. huilo c.

projects through liquid crystal, the language of light. There are no attachments in 5-D. Living here is with integrity and inspires the magic of living in the present—less reliance on future or past. In this realm, one can hear subtle communications that enable the soul consciousness to blossom."

Lola reached out to catch the hearts as they fell. Each of them had a number, one through thirteen.

Ocelotl continued to describe the journey to Lola. "First, we will open the doors of perception. Then, we will pay tribute to the sequence of the equinoxes… a compliment to the mastery of spiritual progression. This is known as the Epocha of Pisces. Afterwards, we will dose those that enter with trance medicines to invigorate the pineal. These are the gate enhancers that assist the experience chamber within a cerebro to discharge a substance known as DMT. It is known to awaken a humano's perception from the fixed state of being. These are known as jaguar medicinas.   After each experience, take a roseheart-key and open one-by-one the portals of consciousness. Study and fuse with the imagery as you pass through. Become one with the phantasmagorias and merge their energies into your mind."

Ocelotl walked down a long golden corridor with Lola.   Heshe bowed and then, together with the Phoenix and Ocelotl, they prepared to open the matrix doors.

The primary doors themselves were astounding to witness. There were four in total and each was a perfect square. Together they looked like one unified image. In the center was a prismatic circle with four tree trunks and their roots conjoined into quadrangles.

An extensive pearly white snake circled the entirety of the doors.   The serpiente held its tail inside its own mouth. The collective image looked like a giant clock with triangular points around the edges.

Lola wondered exactly how to open them. The hearts in heshe's hand were for the gates of ascencia and there were only thirteen. "Ocelotl, any clues on how to open this?" Lola furled their brow.

Ocelotl chuckled. "Of course. There is a chant. I'll recite it with you three times."

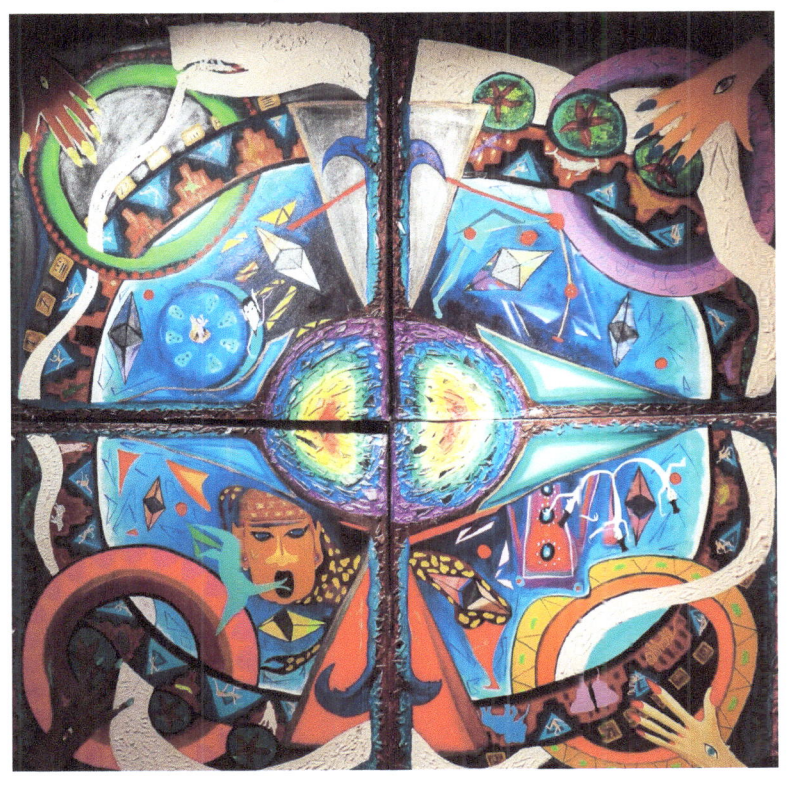

One to thirteen
Open and we shall see
One to four
Gates of this lore
Spinning twirling swirling
Go to the core
Deep inside
You answer why?
Up and up
In and In
Through and through
We shall go
To explore
The ways of being
In a time of new beginnings
One. Two. Three.
Four. Five. Six.
Seven. Eight. Nine.
Ten. Eleven and Twelve.
All hail the 13th gate.
Before it's too late!

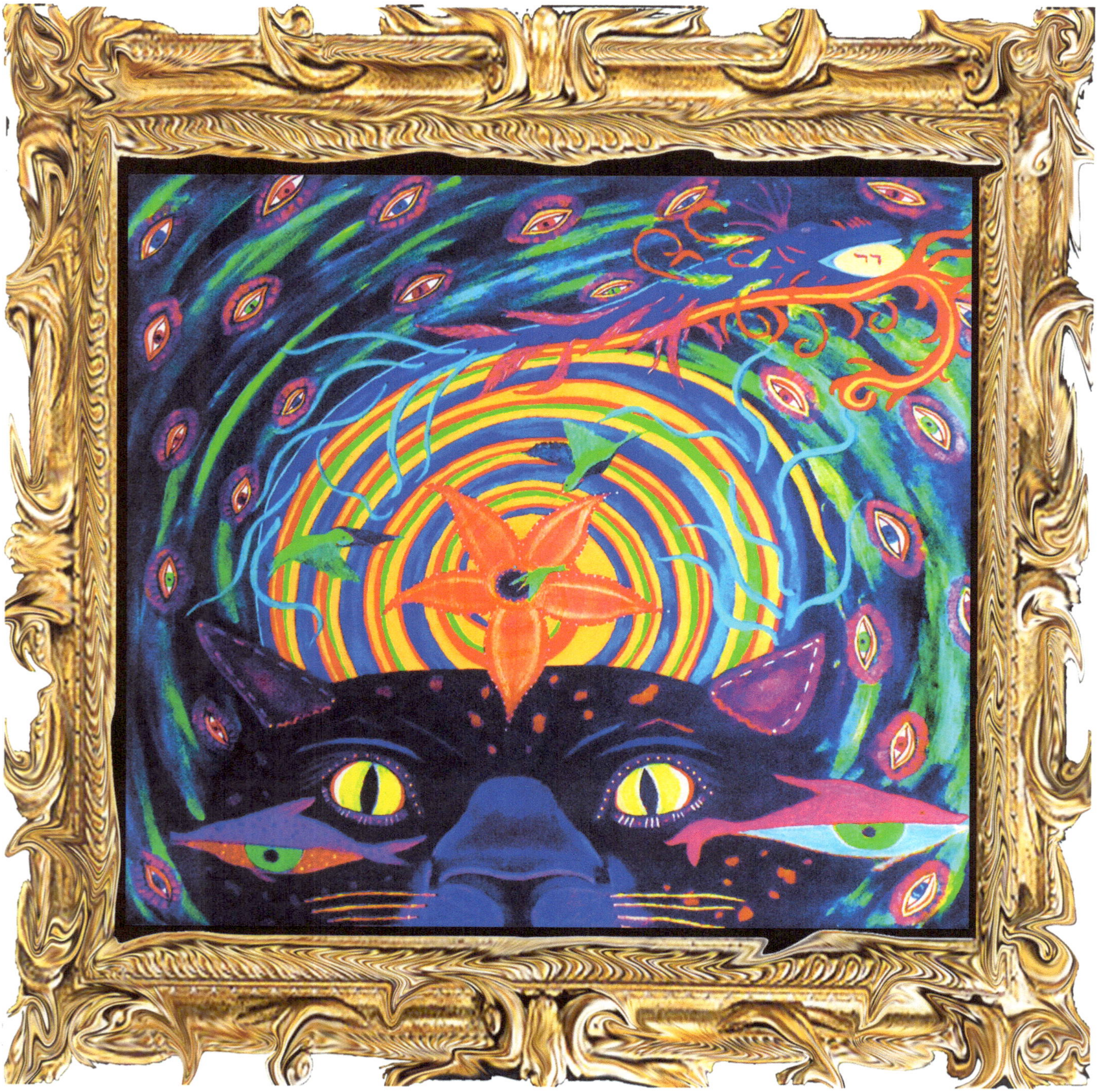

c. huilo c.

*W*ithin seconds the magical rectangles twisted and spiraled together. Then, they suddenly split apart and opened onto a large space. On the furthest wall of the newly opened space was peculiar liquefied vision.

Ocelotl commented on the image. "The humanos... well, indeed all of us really, respond dynamically to imagery in the holosphere. The illusions are not fake or unreal, yet the senses respond to them. They execute cues for the brain, cerebros, to begin producing neurotransmitters. From those substances begin chains of cellular reactions and then subsequent events." Ocelotl paused to let things sink in. "What do you see here Lola?"

Lola looked long and hard at the image. Eeshe's eyes scanned every detail of the picture. There were certainly lots of eyes. Lola dropped into a psychic headspace. Who are you, thought Lola?

"I see... eyes. These are awakened humanos aligned with the All-Seeing-All-Knowing-Eye... referred to as the ALL. There is movement within the image...so I sense change... everything fluctuating. The fish represent dual consciousness and the jaguar is us?"

Ocelotl nodded.

"This is a mirror of the Jaguar Magicians viewing the change. The lotus flower represents an aroused pineal gland. Hummingbirds drink from its necktar... DMT... soul enhancement fluid. This nourishes the mind on how to adapt to the space between worlds... amid planes of consciousness. A spiral of color spins behind the entire painting which is a snake. It is the flying serpent or serpient pluma."

"Have I told you the story of the flying serpent jaguar Lola," asked Ocelotl? "I think this vision activates its archetypal presence. Although, it's not spoken of much in the realm of the humanos it sheds light upon the joining of Tierra and Aire elementos. Transcendence of the mind. Another visualization combines the flying serpiente and the jaguar together, sort of like a flying jaguar with a snake's capacity to descend into the tierra's depths, the underwareworld."

Ocelotl continued discussing the motion of the serpiente in the fantastical portal. "So, here you have a shedding, then a lifting off, conjoined with the capability of seeing in the darkness... into the void. For example, it's how their artisanos conjure a piece of artwork. This portal prepares them and demonstrates the importance during transformation to include sovereignty or union of all life forms and their vital energies.

I presume we are asked, at this point, to invite in and call upon it's principles." Ocelotl continued, "Finally we see the cousins of the Flower Kissers, the Great Flower Eagles revolve and fly into the center. At the same time, they instill joy nectar everywhere.

Into the depths

This way or that?

Into the core

Of Jaguar lore

Fly with the snake

Create the lake

Of inspiration to dream

While awake!

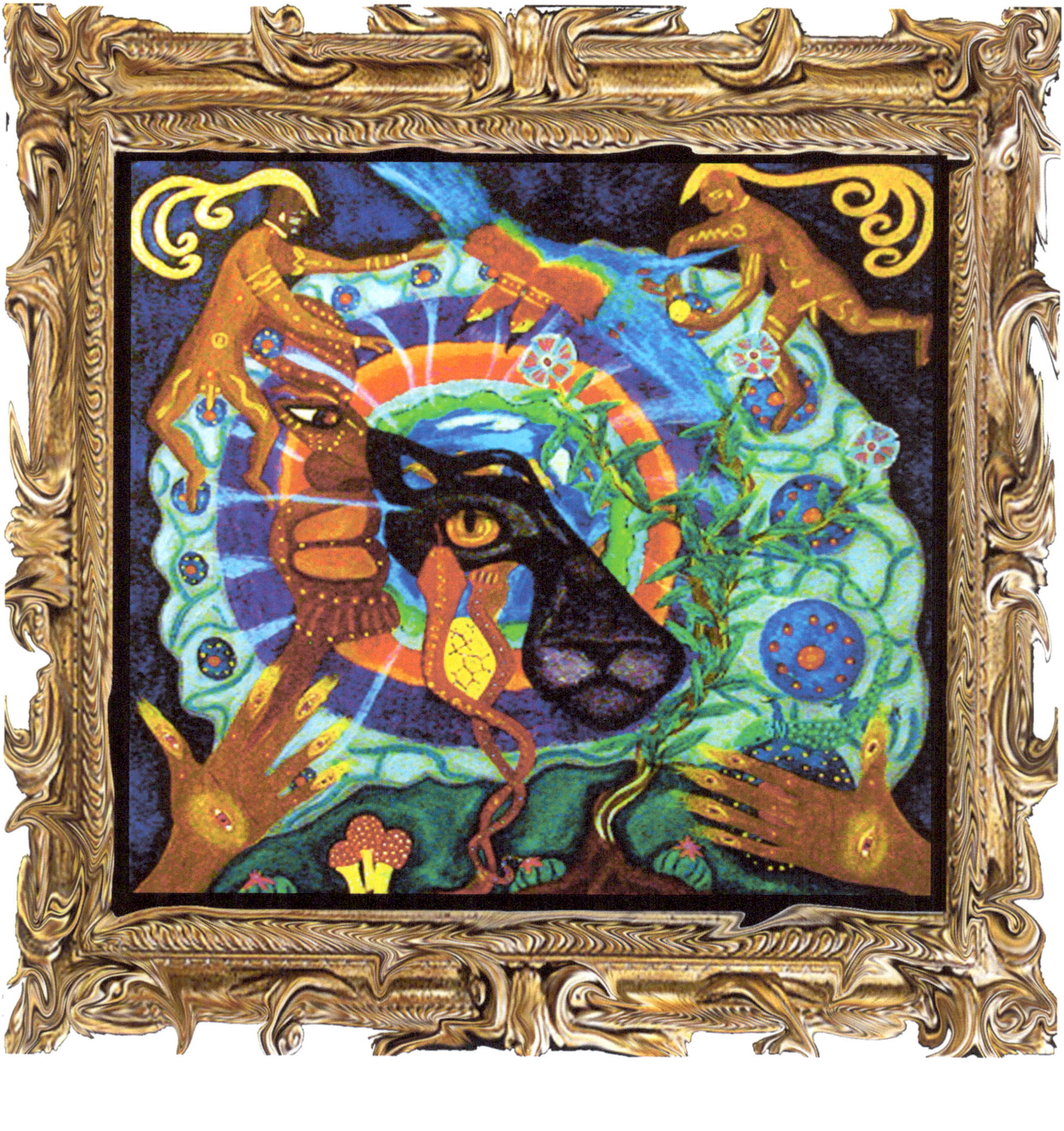

*A*bruptly, the dreamsphere liquefied itself. Poof! Then, it changed again and suddenly they found themselves inside a large, grey puffy mass. It was like being inside a brain or cerebro.

Two snakes emerged from the ground. Mushrooms, cacti and a large vine sprouted from the dirt. At the same time four oversized hands stretched from the corners.

These images work fast, thought Lola. Of course, they are in an active holosphere—an actual change-sphere.

"Ah yes," announced Ocelotl. "Look at these aspects. These plant devas… are offspring of Sera Pheame. We know that the generous tribe of hongos have been healing brain functions in humanos for millennia."

Two shamons joined the vision, piercing through the illusory fabric. They launched laser rays into the dreamsphere. Then, a large brown face with yellow dots joined the illusion. The shamanico spoke. "Inside the mind of the ALL there is no separation."

"My goodness! I believe we are actually inside a humano cerebellum," exclaimed Ocelotl!

"Look! The hands are offering us something. A gift. I'm sensing it's some sort of foresight. Can you see how there's a connection from the Shamanico to the Jaguar and to the plant beings—everything is connected. The snakes are carrying something. They are bringing a golden egg to the center. There are markings on it. May I have a look," asked Lola?

The serpientes paused and suspended in midair. Lola carefully clutched the egg the and examined it. "These are peculiar, I don't recognize them."

The serpientes spoke. "Ssss… tisss the markingsss of the matrixxxsss codesss for DMTeeee… thessseee illumine the optica nerviosa… with ah Day eN A liberationsssss ssequences."

In amazement, Lola watched as the grey walls began to shift color. They shimmered. First, they were green, then red, orange, and at last blue. A huge bird had entered the hallucination and descended into the mind. It had two heads.

"Ah hah! The double headed phoenix. The union of opposites." Ocelotl motioned to Lola to listen carefully. The phoenixes sang.

With two heads, we sing

Glory glory to the bees!

Joining the opposites

We fly into the horizon

Carrying the cosmic egg

New beginning await

Patterns of magic

Come with us

Join the celebration

Of the opening gates!

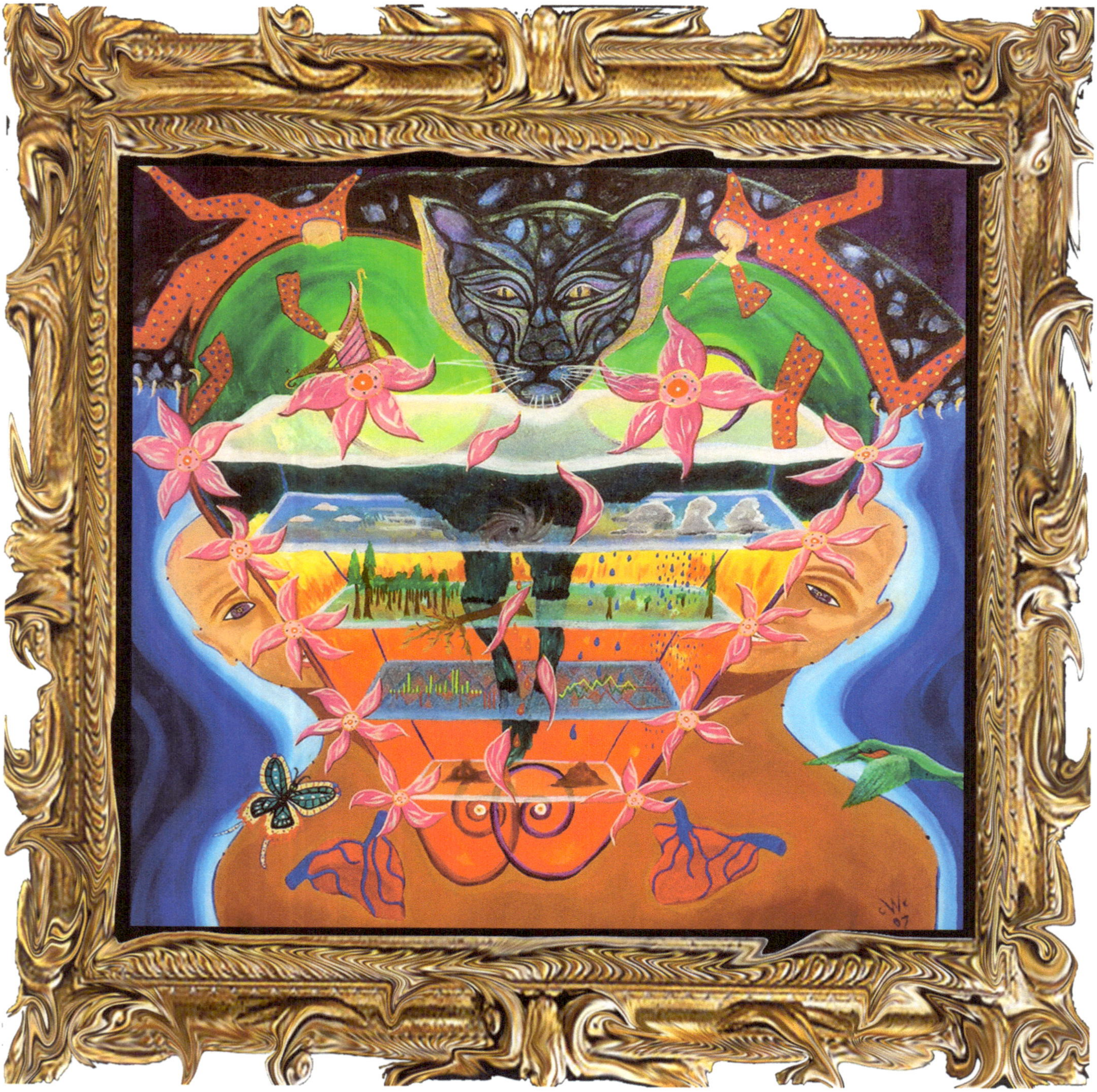

*A*as the medicine or truth was absorbed from each image, the colors blurred and another portal formed. Lola watched as a silhouette formed of a hairless humano. The body was transparent and the heart of the humano was visible through the skin. Lola could see it pulse.

A series of shapes and shades reformed into a stunning, iridescent jaguar. Ocelotl and Lola moved forward to touch the imagery in the holosphere. As they did so, tiers or platforms, formed flowing down from the Jaguar's paws. "Lola, did you ever consider how the blending of the oversoul matrix occurs during a transitionary phase? I think this imagery reveals an important steps to 5-D consciousness. There's a need to merge the dimensions in order for the humano to ascend into the fifth dimensional world," declared Ocelotl.

"I believe that's correct. Yet, I have a feeling this picture also wants to emphasize some of the aspects of various timelines in moving through dimensions. Look at the platforms. They appear to show the duality as oneness. Now that's unique, isn't it?"   Ocelotl stood back and examined the particulars. "One level is volcanic—eruptive consciousness. Then, it moves on from the elemental or tangible form of consciousness to another level. I can also see Gaia's state of fear and fearless consciousness. Moving on, it reveals the magical dream state of 4-D and arrives into the mindfulness of light bodies… This is where they learn to engage and invoke existence beyond linear time through the voice, or, language of light."

Fascinated by the imagery, Lola watched as lotus petals drifted down from the black jaguar's paws. Two shamon danced around spinning the shape of a giant heart. The silhouetted humano split into half, yet it was still joined at the torso. *Yes, of course! They were united at the root of their core being.*

Just then, Ocelotl and Lola were joined by a lovely hummingbird or *flower kisser* and… then? Was it so? Yes! Metamor! The butterfly glided effortlessly around the edges of the beautiful demonstration of 'heart knowing' consciousness.

"Here the image refers to the *Law of Love*. This is the first Gate, Lola." Metamor fluttered around the holosphere. "In this description, Law does not refer to the faux authoritarian control governance of the 3-D realms. Here it simply adjoins to the state of Actions done in alignment to universal disposition within the guidance of the ALL."

Gently, like pages of a book, the flower kissing hummingbird and the butterfly pulled back the petals of a lotus flower at the center.

Lola was exhilarated. Finally, they had arrived at the first gate. This would put things into physical motion.

"I believe now you can use one of those roseheart keys to open this principle," stated Metamor. "Lola, go ahead, you are ready."

Lola reached out and held up a rose to the gate and offered a question, "Who am I now? Who was I? Who will I be?"

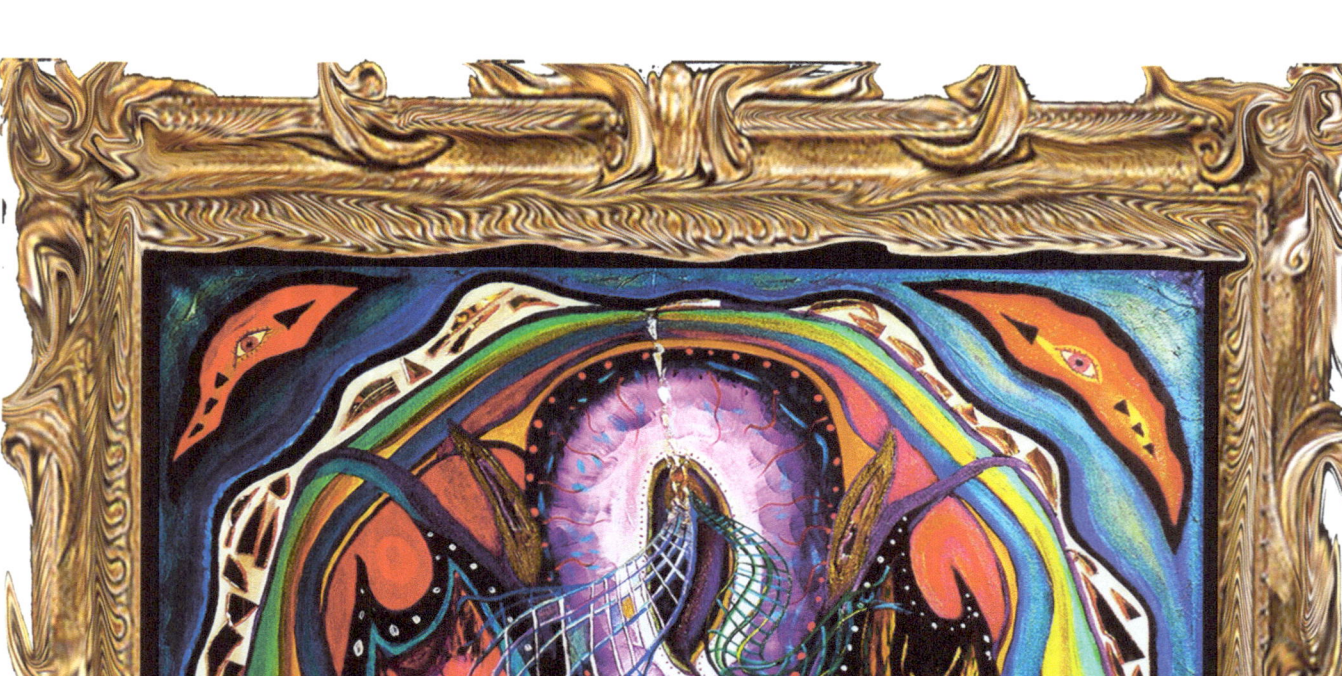

c. huilo c.

$\mathcal{O}$nce again, the shapes changed. Two tiny faeries fluttered in from the parameters of the entryway at gate two.

"Hello Lola! I'm Atomy and this is my counterpart Molecula. We represent the significance and truth of the first dimension."

With that, the faeries tapped on two colorful spirals in the center of the gateway. A large mirror emerged and revealed a humano head, but with no face. Then it split, and shattered into two separate and distinct faces which swirled away from the center of original, faceless head.

"Wowza! Duality consciousness made real, gurrrlll," giggled Lola.

"Humanos are encoded with keys to galvanize their evolutionary state. This is the story that resonates the fusing of positive and negative energies. Of polarity and magnetizing its force. Rather than to defy this obstensible, disuniting, yet natural energy, it is actually one to *integrate*—it holds universes together. Think graviteeee," shared Molecula.

"While so many of the humanos and jaguar magicians may agonize in the tension of this locus, the gate is an invitation to appreciate discomfort that can bring greater appreciation for joy. It cannot be easily resisted. Sometimes, the agony can remove obstacles and release energy for understanding the nature of life and the core mind of universal intelligence. The All within the All. And the All within the ALL." The two heads in the mirage began to chant.

It's not a duel!

Don't be so cruel!

Magnetize!

Polarize!

Solarize.

Union of opposites

Bridger of worlds!

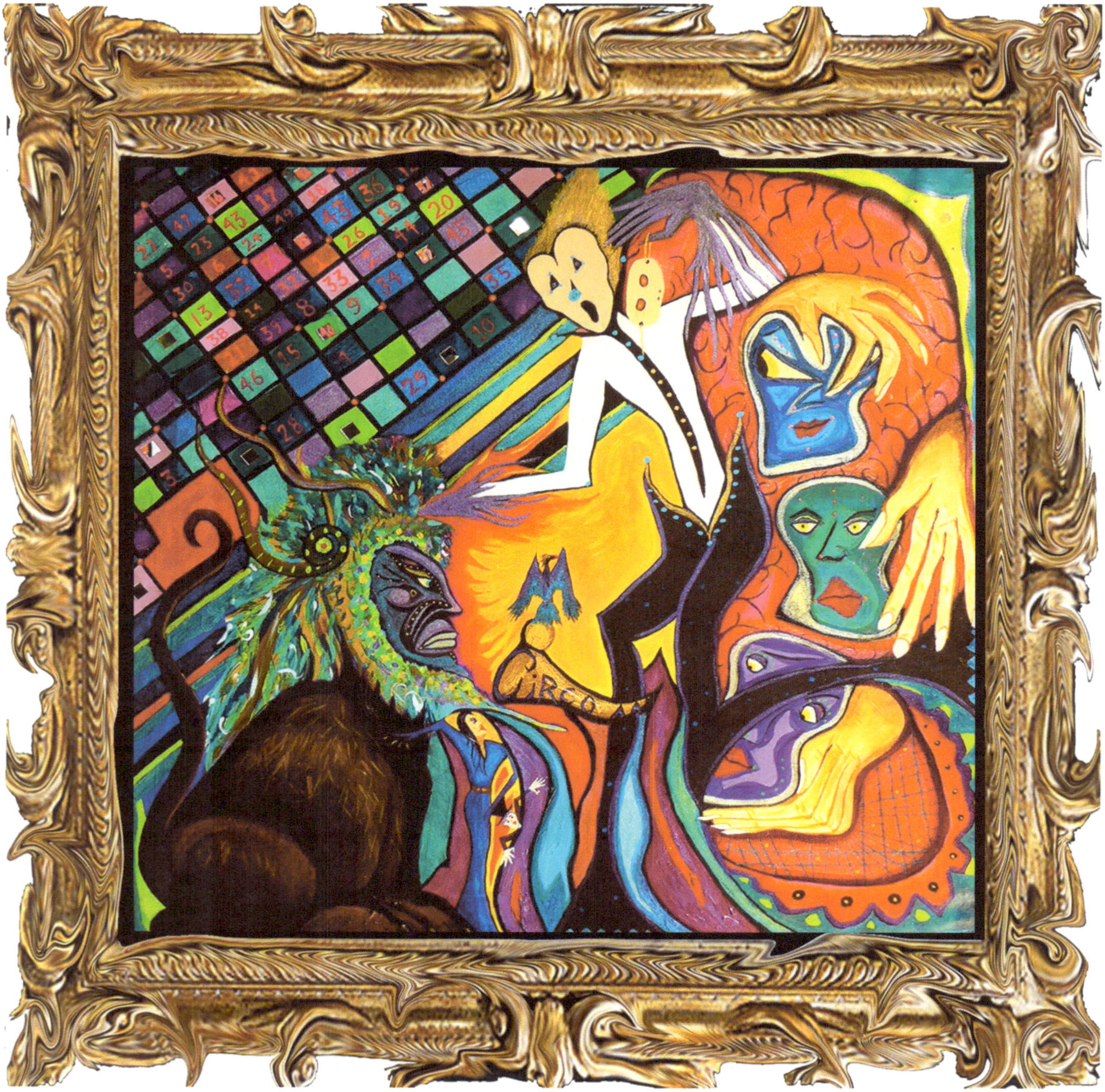

*A*fter the duality generation concluded the integration of its principle, source pulled back upon itself into a unified field—the profile of oneness. Lola looked around as the mysts disappeared, and it seemed Ocelotl had vanished. In the meantime, heshe regarded their surroundings.

The entrance to a Circo tent flapped in a breeze. A familiar face, Mister Minutes peered from the folds of the doors.

I wonder what Mr. Minutes is doing here? Heshe approached the Circo and as they did, an enormous majestic lion materialized.

"He... he... hello! I'm Lola. Are you a guardian of this gate," asked Lola?

"Greetings magician. Yes. It is the entry and place of *Resolution of Emotional Motion*. I am Galantri, cousin to Whitelionmeetsbuffalowomon, whom I believe you have walked with on your travels?"

"Ah yes! Indeed, I have. I just opened the gate of duality and somehow arrived here. So, is this gate three?"

"Well, perhaps. I'm not sure the sequencing is the same for everyone. However, this is the realm of potencia. It addresses how mental motion is increased through focused will. And, in doing so, it takes great courage. Let us join my friends Skeletal and Mr. Minutes."

Lola joined the others and watched as Skeletal pulled four masks out of Galantri's head! "Excuse me, but what is happening with those masks?"

"One of the attributes of this realm, is the blending of the plant, reptile, insect and animal kin-doms. These are the companions of humanos. They all share ah Day eN A matrix codes. Yet in order for there to be emotional activity and thereby increase potential, one must come to accept that these kin species. Humanos must consider the stellar vibrations of these creatures as grander at times than their own, and certainly not lesser. Increased empathy for all beings! They carry with them wisdom teachings from higher planes of existence."

Mr. Minutes ran outside the tent. "Remember how to jump timelines? Like when, sequences of linear events are able to merge with spatial time sequencing and move between parallel realities? Well, one can also jump levels of consciousness. The superconscious mind is like a huge computer. Various levels of ah Day eN A activate through each gate that humanos traverse. As you know, Lola, you are traveling through them right now and engaging each one as a mirror of yourself."

Skeletal continued, "These masks I removed from Galantri embody parts of the ego mind. They must perish in order to transcend gate number two of consciousness. Sexuality, gender rivalry and possessive energies that hide complete unity with the divine are dissolved."

"Ok, I get it. The mental motion field and the *Law of Pure Potential*! Then I offer the roseheart key to transcend to next level," declared Lola.

"Yes, but let me add one more element. The numbers. Remember each number provides translation to the quantum equations of existence. 7, 8, 9, 3, 2, 1, 00.11, etc. Travel well magician." Galantri bid farewell to Lola.

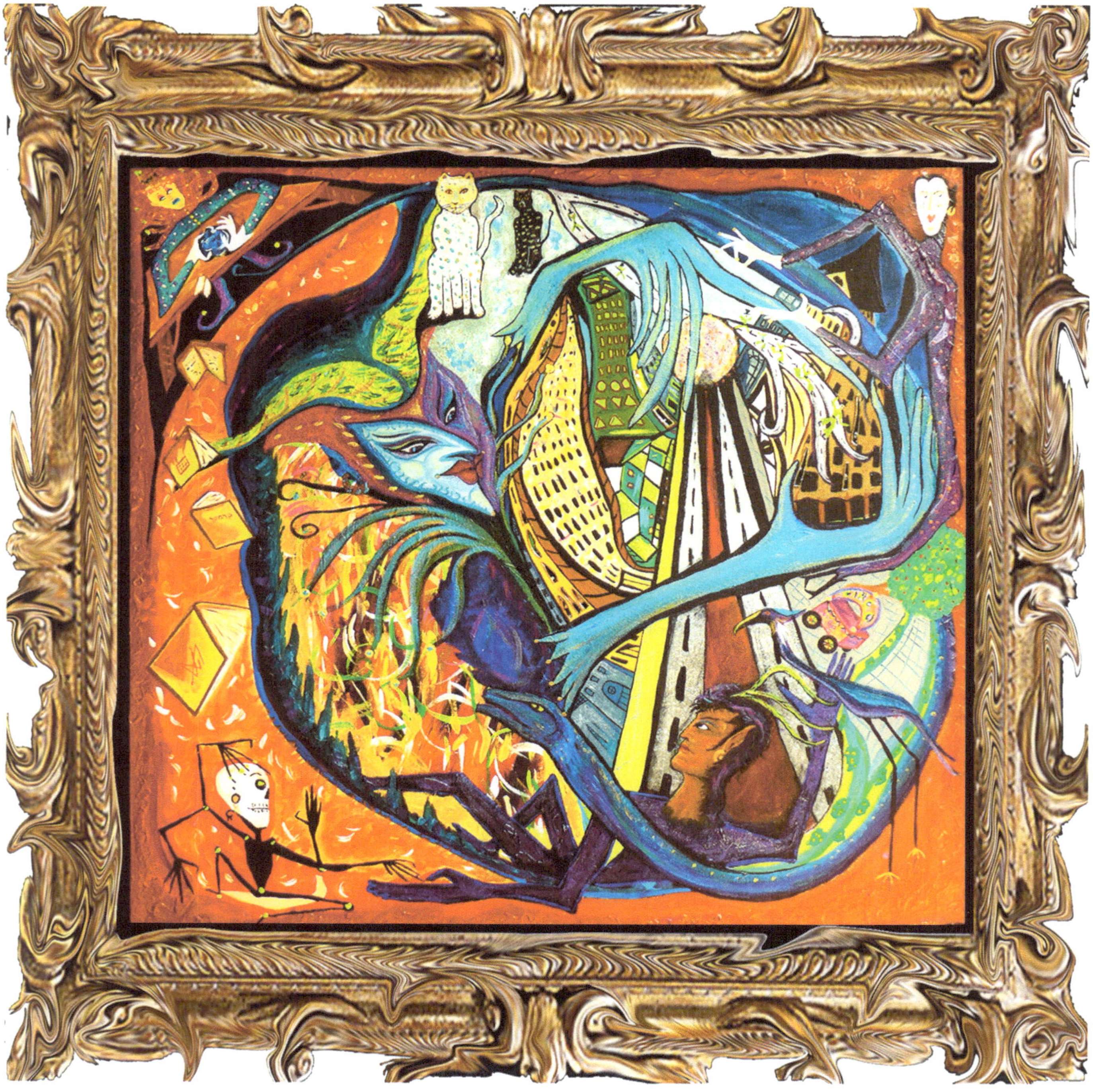

c. huilo c.

304

Lola was mesmerized by the ability of the gates to dissolve from one into another. And now, the last field of unity vanished and changed into a citayscape with a narrow road.

"Ah yes, the long and delicate path to unified consciousness. Welcome Lola to the 3rd realm. I am Unificata. I am the merged self from the first Gate. You've traveled through physical, emotional and now this is where the mental realm focuses on free will. Let's join the others, Skeletal is here, WhiteLion, Pantera and a cousin to Swansong, Heronia."

First, it appeared as a chaotic mirage, shimmering and changing constantly. Then, books, lots of them, were tossed by a Sakred Klown while the jester was spinning the blue planeta upon the desktop. Lola heard a band playing crazy tunes off in the distance.

"What are the flying books about," asked Lola?

"I'll take this one Unificata. They are the books of wisdom. Tomes of revelation. Isn't that right, Payaso Pyneal," asked Skeletal?

"Weeeeee… These tomes activate structured thought. Focused will. Determination. Devotion. For milliena wizards have gathered tales of probabilities on how to how to recreate the world into an altered image… with a more balanced grid."

The energy shifted. At the end of the road, a portal of transformation opened. It was similar to the one in that Rosey had led them to in the Citay. Numerous humanos walked upon a silvery flare into the fingers of Unificata. In the meantime, Skeletal caught book after book and tossed them into Lola's hands.

"Here, this one's on alchemia. This one's on geomatria. This ones on tarota. This one's on crystal codes, your old friend Ametist Mal o Kite wrote it! And here's one on plant devas by Sera Pheame. A book of poetry by Wizard Weezel. Oh, my goodness and here's one by Dusty Miller, I thought it was out of print!" Skeletal shouted off title after title until there were thousands of books in a pile.

The records rose up into the air forming stack after stack, like a small city of towers. Lola tumbled to the ground from the weight of them all. Madness was at hand, yet it also seemed to congeal some sort of logic at the same time, the idea of wisdom alchemizing thoughts into ideas.

"This is the place where humanos emerge and become aware of the decrees pertaining to soul consciousness. The boulevard in the citay is a pathway to the gate of reasoning. One by one, they step into the reformation of rational, logical, and analytical thought. Then, the gate opens and the hypnotic trance of ego dominated decisions are transmuted," declared Unificata.

Ocelotl had reappeared and was gently escorting humanos onto the pathway.

Awake, dear one, awake!

At long last, open your mind.

Awake! Abandon your sleep of illusion.

It is foolish to sleep all the time.

"Join us on the passageway of self-discovery and let us open the fourth gate! Lola use the next roseheart key, here, now," shouted Ocelotl!

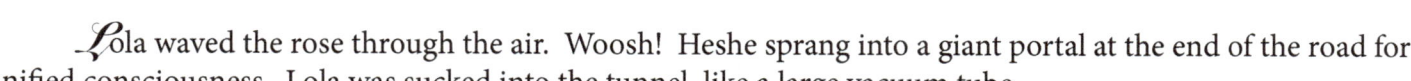

$\mathcal{L}$ola waved the rose through the air. Woosh! Heshe sprang into a giant portal at the end of the road for unified consciousness. Lola was sucked into the tunnel, like a large vacuum tube.

"Manu eira mana…manu eira mana… manu eira mana…" Voices chanted in the darkness. It was pleasantly warm with a soft breeze as heshe glided into the unknown. Light slowly returned to Lola's vision revealing an odd landscape of doors and billowing storm clouds that generated fierce lightening.

Ocelotl suddenly reappeared. "Well Lola, we are at gate five, I believe? I imagine the background chant is initiating a discharge from the Cosmic Shield. This is the place where the omnipotent nature of creation and the *Law of Free Will* converge."

Out of the shadows arrived a portentous figure. With emerald skin and a gorgeous PeeKock wrapped

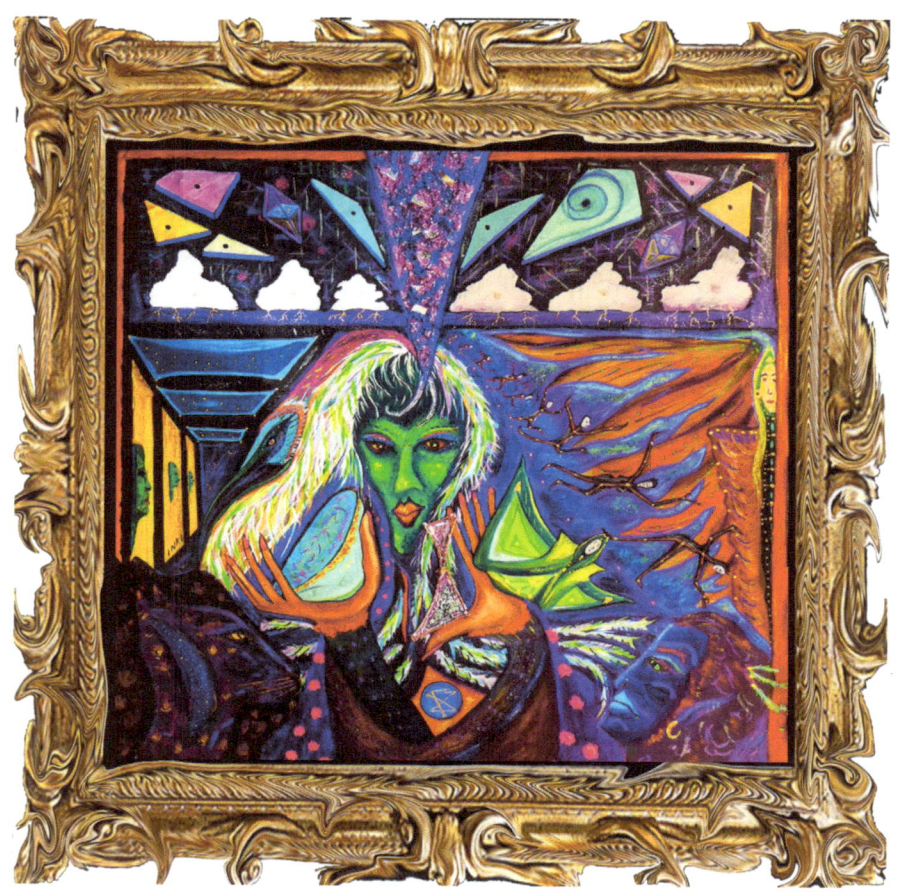

around their neck, the eccentric being was accompanied by several other mystical individuals.

"Hello I am 'EirA'. I am one of the Emerald Guardians. Here we focus Free Will and its innate ability to create a Kozmic Event Horizon. This is the area where universal magnetic unions are invigorated into tangible illusions. Some may refer to this also as the *Law of Attraction*. However, it is so much more." EirA looked to her side. "Won't you join me, Amor Raea Flaame? Let us tell a tale of this gate's ability for acceleration of consciousness."

Immediately they were joined by a female bodied shemon who had rose violet flames shooting from her sides. She seemed in a deep trance. As she waved her hands three golden doors appeared to the right. Lola watched bright green, luminescent faces surface from the unique portals.

"These are the openings of choice. Self of Obvious. Self of Sufficient. Self of Sustainable. Together they spawn into motion of the *Law of One*. When activated, they combine and create the morphogenic field which strengthens sensitivity to the *Law of Correspondence*. It is here one comes into alignment with circumstance and learning." The bird that wrapped around EirA's head observed Lola closely. EirA continued, "Also woven into this realm is the *Law of Order* which determines time, space, function and boundaries between universes. Together they create an environment to manifest and enable specific planes of residence for each species and how each is allowed to experience life. All are revealed as a circumstance generated by itself."

"What are all those pieces or cubes behind you floating in the air," asked Lola?

"Those are from the Partiki Grid. They cloak us and connect one to parallel universes where anything and everything and nothing are all happening at the same time while not happening at all! Bahahahahah!" EirA seemed quite bemused at our naivety.

Ocelotl sensed a potential point of confusion for Lola. The master jaguar magician elaborated, "What is referred to here is similar to our work with ah Day eN A and the reverent being known as, Whitelionmeetsbuffalowomon. However, this is also being activated by scalar waves and a hydroplasma beam."

Ocelotl pointed to a large rift in the horizon that was lit up with glowing shards of mirrors and crystals. "Can you see that beam descending flashing a strange light? That ray opens twelve dimensions and thus only the thirteenth is left to unfurl. But we aren't there yet. Look there's a fae arriving!"

They were joined by yet another magical being. A sparkling jade, winged being fluttered down and landed on the shoulder of EirA. Meanwhile, the reverent priestess's hands raised up into the air and crisscrossed them before her chest. EirA held a turquoise goblet in their left hand and in the right she grasped a bulbous device of some sort.

The feathered faerie spoke to them. "Greetings everyone! I'm of the fluttering fae, and am called, Auntie Karana." The magical elfin being surveyed her surroundings. "What a fabulous authority this gate embraces for it has summoned the great Choirs of Venus and the intelligences of compassion. Together we bring forth the energy of divine kundalini.

Do you remember the story of kundalini shared by Transmuta the serpent long ago, Lola? This form of union and awakening is the All within the All and All is in ALL. Here we accelerate consciousness to interchange between realms easier, and therefore, more beings affecting at-will event constructs." Auntie Karana buzzed closer to Lola. She hovered radiantly and smiled at the jaguar magician.

"This is necessary in order to increase the velocity of vibration before one can continue to the higher realms. Yes and, most importantly, we must do so before activating the highest level of oscillations to the order of the hummingbirds."

Auntie Karana gestured to the horizon. "The great flower kisser of the heavenly golden nectars only serves those who sustain a frequency higher than even our dear Amor Raea Flaame." The dancing faerie flew to join her friend, Amor.

"Then so it is! Here, with Ocelotl! Lola! Amor Raea Flaame! Auntie Karana! We drink from the chalice of inspiration, the nourishing divine juice, 'Tis. Now, I shake in my right hand the chronoglass and thus activate the grids, waves and universes of innovation."

EirA motioned to her left. "Come forward genies of liberation!" Then, out of the hydroplasmic beam, darted several sprites. Each ran up to Lola's forehead and pressed on heshe's third-eye portal implanting the codes of this gate.

"The Soul Matrix of the fifth Gate is now open! Proceed to level six please, if you will." EirA and the others vanished.

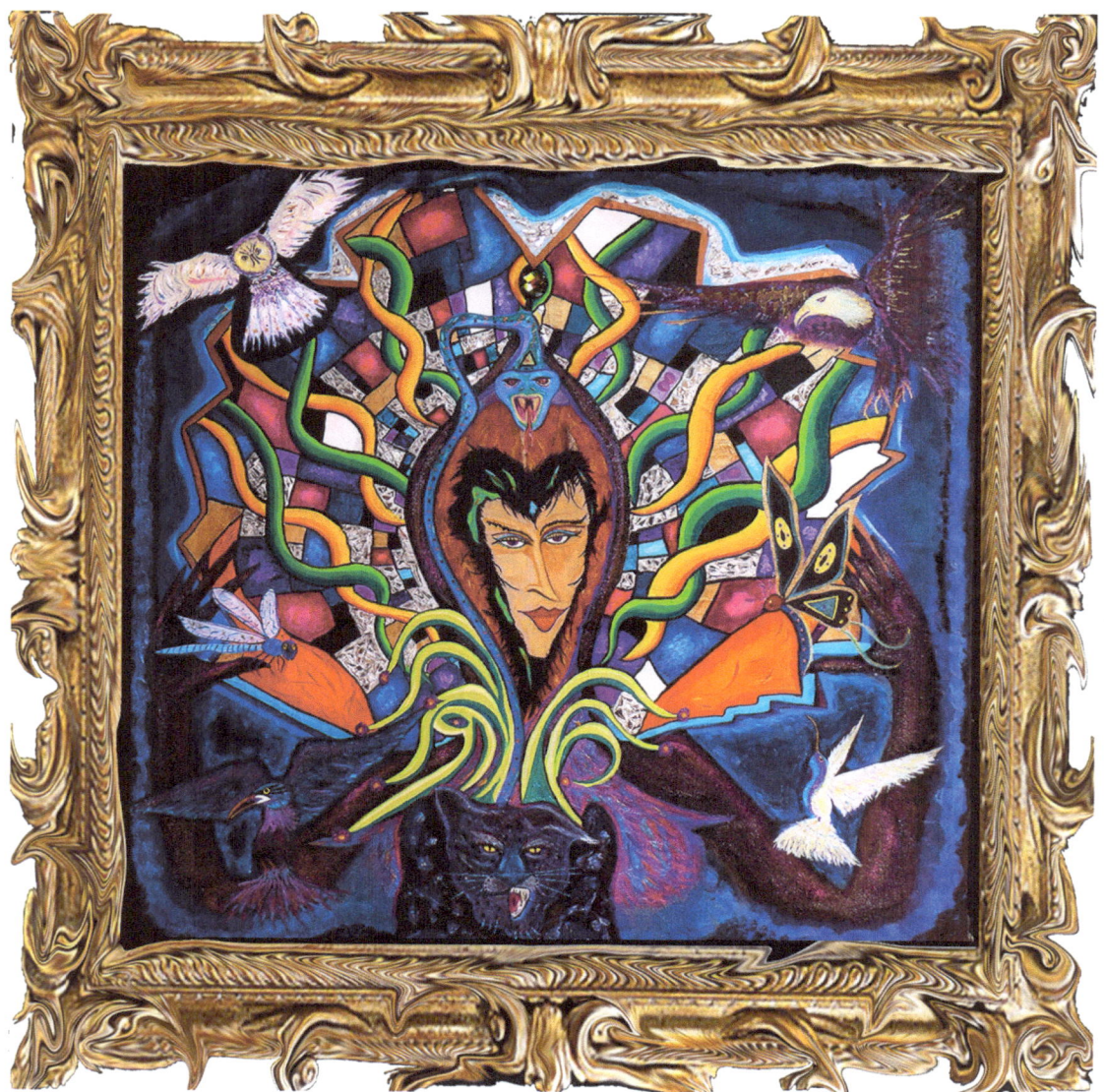

$\mathcal{S}$econds later, Lola was jolted into darkness. Then, heshe rested into a suspended animation. Surrounded by kaleidoscopic images which intermittently shattered and fused in the void. All at once, they stopped moving and formed a massive grid.

"Welcome to the sixth gate Lola! I am Kriz A. Lis. I am attributed to be the bridger of the awakened state and the releaser of the veil between higher dimensions. You have once again been brought to an influential demesne referred to as the Meta-tronia channel. During this activation, we are joined by the other keepers of the fourth realm. Let us welcome them."

Leopardo crawled forth from the dark shadows. "I offer energy awareness and reclaiming power while inviting in the secrets of sensitivity—sensuality to the subtle.   I direct attention to the elusive, the mystic power of darkness by which exists within the great black void, the cores from which all come and all return. The skill of shapeshifting from into formlessness and other shapes will allow one to transgress gate to gate."

The large felina sat in the darkness and examined the sky, looking for something. Suddenly, they were joined by a great white owl which soared elegantly from the stars.

"Exquisite, Oracula has joined us," affirmed Leopardo.

Lola gazed with wonder at the fabulous plumage of the owl.

"I bring the art of the messenger. The anecdote of sight beyond illusion which engages the expertise to retrieve all aspects of the soul… and to move them forward. This is the realm of how to *know to see*, and *see to know*. Seeing the darkness into shape is what I mirror here. I bring the spirit of the Gaia-walkers from long ago, ancient future past."

Kriz A. Lis lifted her voice and said, "I may add, that liberating the super-consciousness by purifying and strengthening will ultimately increase the electric charges of this crystal grid which surrounds us now."

Hundreds of mirrors sparkled while strands of ah Day eN A flowed through them. "Ah yes, attention everyone RavenA has flown in, bless her heart," thundered Kriz A. Lis.

"Quite the gathering Kriz you have here. Delighted to join." The aviary being stayed somewhat hidden in the shadows. "Well let's see what I can add to this black hole, errr… void. Ah hah! I bring forth the earned right, having passed through five gates, of the right to experience things beyond belief. Here we bend and fold time and space, alchemizing the form to formless and back again, the bridge of the non-physical. I invoke the ceremonies to engage intentions to the ultimate destination of Odin, where lies the wisdom of the trickster realm. I reveal my secret name now, Morrigana."

Lola quietly gasped. Morrigana, how similar that name was to heshe's divine twin, Morgano. Hmmm… "What a potent group. Look, here comes yet another!" Lola pointed to another large bird arriving to the circle.

Suil-na-Greine spread his wings and puffed, "Ah yes, I bring vision from the uppermost realms. The magic of expansiveness and new beginnings as we program the 144 Krystal grid into full potential. We instill it with the freedom of oneness."

Everyone watched in amazement as the vibrant colors in the grid around Kriz A. Lis whirled wildly in the air and gathered more and more momentum with each guest's magic.

Lola heard a soft buzz in the air and immediately recognized dragonflies, the messengers of Sera Pheame. "Welcome dragonias!"

Magic song flight.
Perception self.
Conditioned possibilities freed.
Transcendence dance.
Breaking illusions.
Water and air.
Overcoming identity of one's 'self'.
Come forth great faerie realms.

Finally, the whimsical assembly was joined by yet another, a gorgeous white hummingbird, flower kisser. "Hellos! I am Herzia the carrier of higher frequency and stopper of time. And joining me is dear, Metamor!"

"Oh my! Oh my! Dear ally," shouted Lola.

"Let us advance those that make it this far from the earthly Gaica matters to astounding momentum of beauty, balance and delight! At this gate, one enters the world of the soul-illuminating and soul-consciousness. By engaging this spacetime, one becomes more of the you!"

The dazzling albino flew to the center of the group. "Kriz. A. Lis! The stellar, ultimate changeling. You teach the mastery of completely heart-rendering of ah Day eN A from one form to another!"

Whistles and cheers emanated from the group in celebration of the activation of Gate Six on behalf of the ascencia codigos for the tribe of humanos. Then, there was another surprise burst, Transmuta, the serpiente, arrived to connect the others.

"Sssssssooo good to sssssee everyone. Come with me now to the top of the pyramid…the sssseventh gate awaits! Come Lola! Come now!"

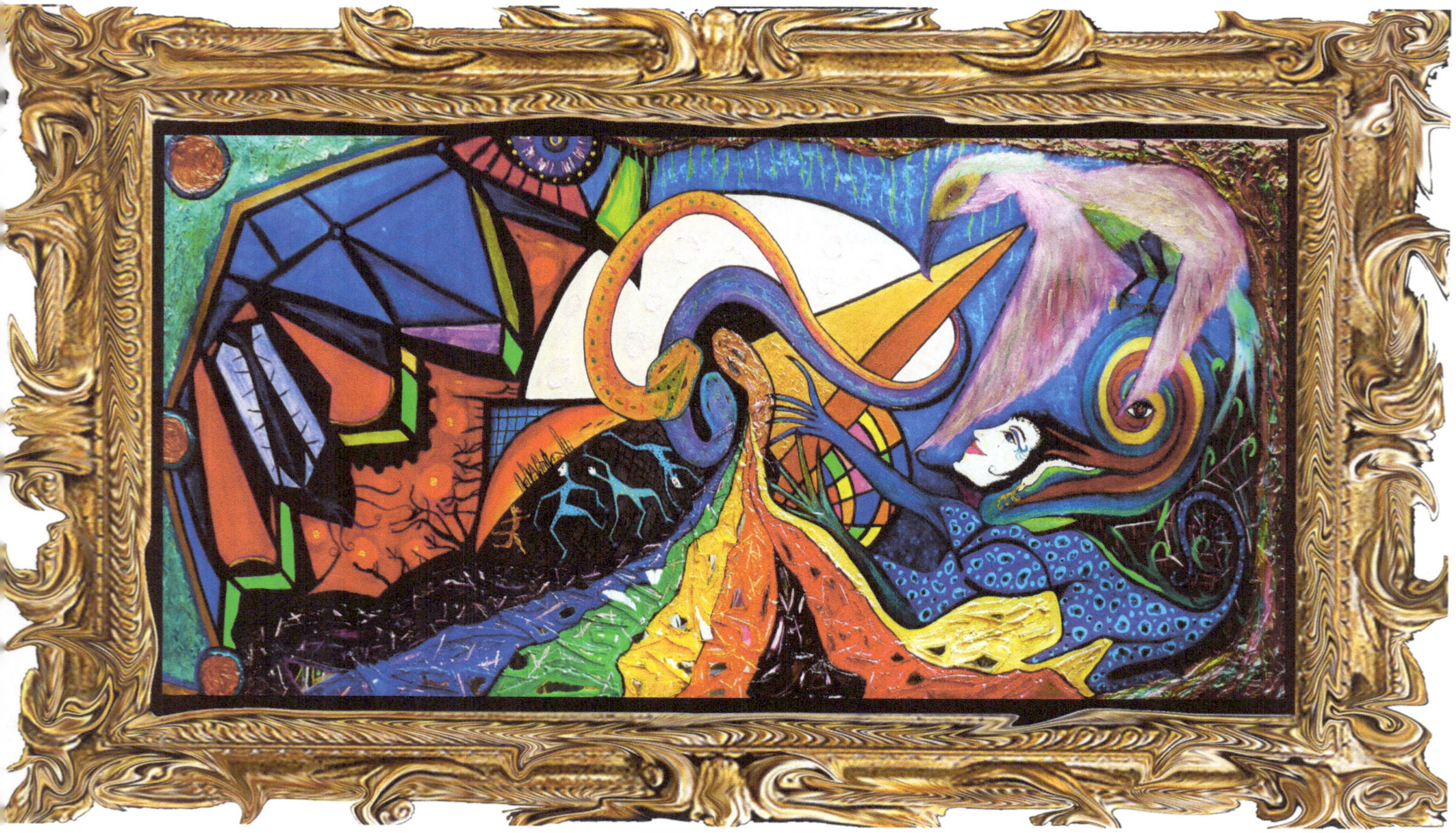

c. huilo c.

Lola felt as engaged as ever knowing that this was all leading towards the 13th gate. Now, heshe waved yet another roseheart key into the air and waited for a new image to appear.

Bright flashes of light and then a series of silhouetted dancers appeared in front of a brilliant fiery orange background. They seemed to be calling something down from the sky. Then, slowly over the horizon, Luna arrived, pearly white and full, followed by a shimmery phoenix who flew down from the heavens. The dancers had summoned a magnificent forum to the scene. The huge eccentric being descended majestically to join the others. The being seemed to be assembled from large angular zones or parts.

"I am Septad the awakener of the 7th level, the 7th gate, and the 7th heaven. Thank you all for inviting me on this quest to integrate the laws of healing, honesty, synthesis, and the *Law of the Three into One*. I present these as directives rather than dictates. In order to manifest may we summon the will of the inhabitants of the urban jungles on Gaia, the golden pyramid, the Arbol de Vida who holds the seeds of life, and our dear ally CoYotl?"

Out of the mysts from behind the Arbol de Vida strolled a large feline. Leopantcoujago Azul whispered, "Ooooo…yes. Greetings everyone. As we invoke the principles and the appealing gifts within the 7th gate, I am reminded that healing brings faith. Honesty brings integrity. Synthesis brings oneness. The Law of 3 brings union."

On a distant horizon, additional dancers appeared. They brought elements from the urban jungle. Coyotl joined them and began to leap and prance.

Searching
Loving
Knowledge
Wisdom
Unity
Contentment
Wonderment
From poverty and absolute nothingness…
to cosmic consciousness…

Septad gazed upon the vision. "Lola join us as, if you will, as we summon the enchantment of Three into One. Come forth, triad of serpientes! Cousins of our friend Transmuta! Espiritu! Cuerpito! Almama! Rise from the rubble of the phoenix fyres!"

Then, unexpectedly, Phoenix plummeted from the sky. "Seven. Seven. Seven. We accentuate your rainbow coalescence into the portal of the pineal and build strength into the perfection inertia. Divine trinity we invite you to swirl the planetary forces of gravitation, electromagneticas, and crystalline awareness."

Lola shared a revelation. "In the domain of the humanos, 7 is attributed to the number of planetas they can actually see in their solaria view. I believe it's also the number of the crown chakra. Their music is aligned with 7 notes of a scale as well… what a lovely number."

The snakes surged forth from the rubble and formed into one unified being which spiraled around the Golden Pyramid. They began to integrate new strands of ah Day eN A.

The resplendent tree shook its branches. "Revolutionary restoration of the whole consciousness rise up! Attune with the love, wisdom, and power of Divinity, so that error, confusion, and bigotry can be swept away." Arbol de Vida dispersed their lifeseeds into the Kosmica of the 7th gate.

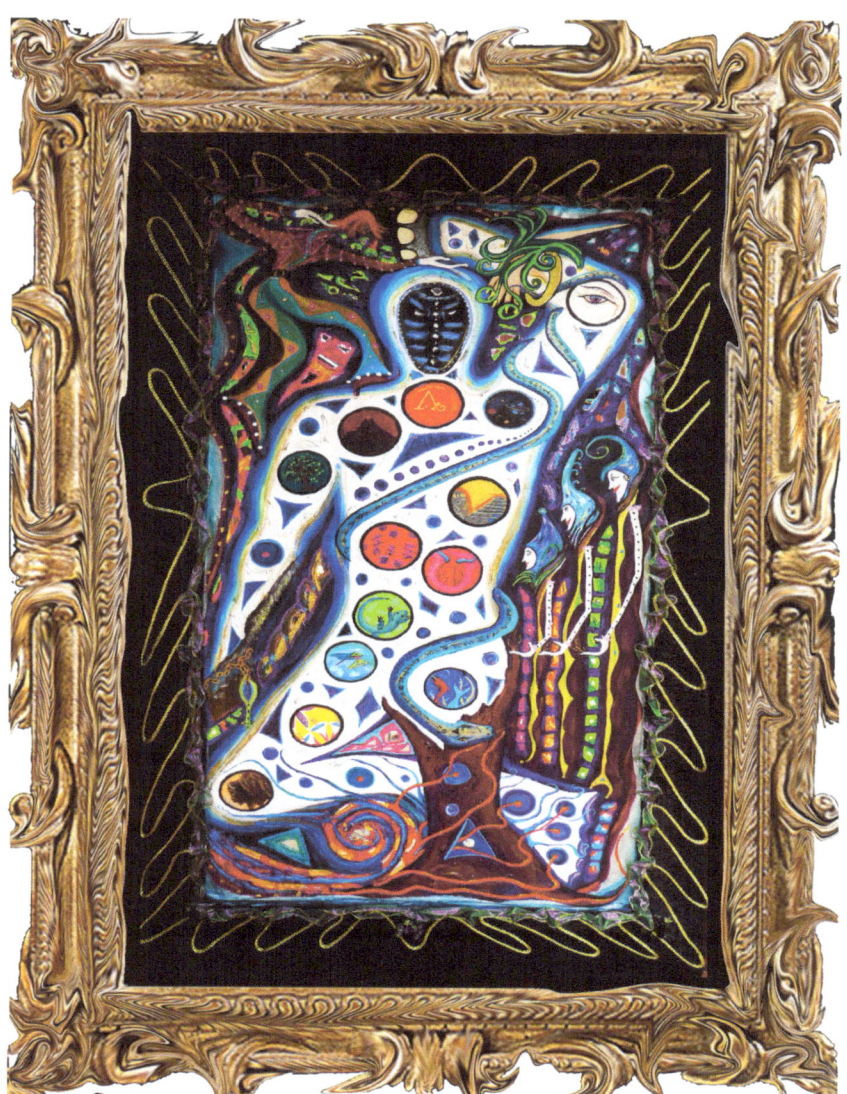

𝒯here was a bright flash of light and then, within moments, Lola entered a large galaxy filled with floating spheres. Golden threads of light zigzagged from the furthest reaches of the giant void. Immediately, out of the darkness emerged a large white figure who began walking toward Lola.

As it got closer, heshe noticed it had strange spots on it and unusual appendages. One hand was of what looked like that of an elephant and the other resembled a horse or goat's. Its feet were not like the feet of any sort Lola had seen. One was similar to the trunk of a tree with bark and all! The other was fin-like, akin to a seal.

In any case, the being stationed itself in front of Lola and launched various postures, as if signaling heshe to do the same. Then, adding to Lola's confusion, three apparitions were swept onto the scene, white-faced, tall, spindly creatures. Each held a small flame in their hand.

"We are the 3-Sirians. Come forward and join us. We are awaiting for another, known as the Flamer, Rubio."

"This is the 8th gate," asked Lola. "Eight symbolizes infinity. It's such a lovely number."

At last, the remaining invitee appeared. Blonde and handsome Rubio was dressed in wild, swirling patterned garments.

"Lola here we are at the resonant tone of the 8 as you say. Infinity. Yes, and in that infinity, is the interweaving tales of ah Day eN A. Without a doubt, there is much you have gathered along your travels about these mysterious codified strands, yet, here we integrate and synthesize it, and weave its story together. At higher levels of consciousness each being, participant, in the great mystery, fully understands there is no separation. Residing inside each humano's ah Day eN A is the story of many things."

"Yes, I have heard many interpretations and magics of ah Day eN A. It is quite fascinating and its depth of potential is incredible. Everything is a part of everything else. The first strand of ah Day eN A is the essence of the ALL within the ALL. Of course, that carries over to all strands and planes of consciousness, right," inquired Lola?

"Reverent Magician, Lola, you are correct! Yet, even more so, these are planes of consciousness that one must surpass. In doing so, one mirrors their strengths into the world of Gaia, and of course, to your special allies, the jaguar magicians. Those that resonate with the lambda codes are bridging spheres of the physical and essence mind.

Look at all these circles of life. Mammalia is cousin to WhiteLionMeetsBuffaloWomon. Your old friend the Lizard, DreamWeaver has joined us as well. Cousins to your friend, Metamor, the mariposas. The flower kissers and friends of Flora. Arbol de vidas! Estrellas! Whalens, delfinas and even the Merstarians. The patternas that form and reform life from 3-D to all dimensions are all interrelated together.

Therefore, when one harms one, it harms the self. Ah, here comes Gaia with an olive branch to remind us of the total peace that comes with this dimension."

The 3-Sirians spoke up, "Nothing is random in life. It is all precious. Every aspect of it. In this dimension is the *Law of Chemical Affinity*. The *Law of Cohesion*. The *Law of Discipline*. The *Law of Expansion*. The *Law of Magnetic Impulse*. The *Law of Order of Creation*.

At present, so many humanos on Gaia's planeta struggle with meaning of life, the why of existence. The illusion of separation from the divine. By existing—one simply exists. No Right. No Wrong. As an ally to the double-spirits you have wished for them to awaken and conjoin to the greater good of all beings. True? These allies bring forth suspended animation of the realized balanced brain… non-dualistic consciousness. They are also messengers to quicken the vibration.

These gates are open to all. Yet—remember these sacred laws and assimilate them into your daily practice. It will bring forth the environment for change. This is the realm of inter-dependence."

"Here comes Transmuta to surround the formal DeeNAe with the magic of integration. These ever-flowing energies contain an affinity for one another and grow with each other. They each have a divine discipline they follow, an order of completion. Each is part of an ever-expanding range of possibilities in life and form. Each is spawning with the influence of magnetic impulse, atom to molecule and on and on." Rubio sang and danced around the totemic being.

The flamer Rubio continued, "Magnificent! And all fall into the domain for the Order of Creation. The great mystery that it all is, has order. Each strand has the directive to carry through with the manifestation and form conscious, vegetated material."

"Wow, truly humbling." Lola sat still, taking it all in.

The 3-Sirians walked in a circle. "We are reaching toward the critical point of ascension where there is more light than darkness—not as in it is more good or less bad… just a higher vibration where new and different things are experienced and the density of fear is released. Now, Lola we send you off to gate 9. Bless you on your journey!"

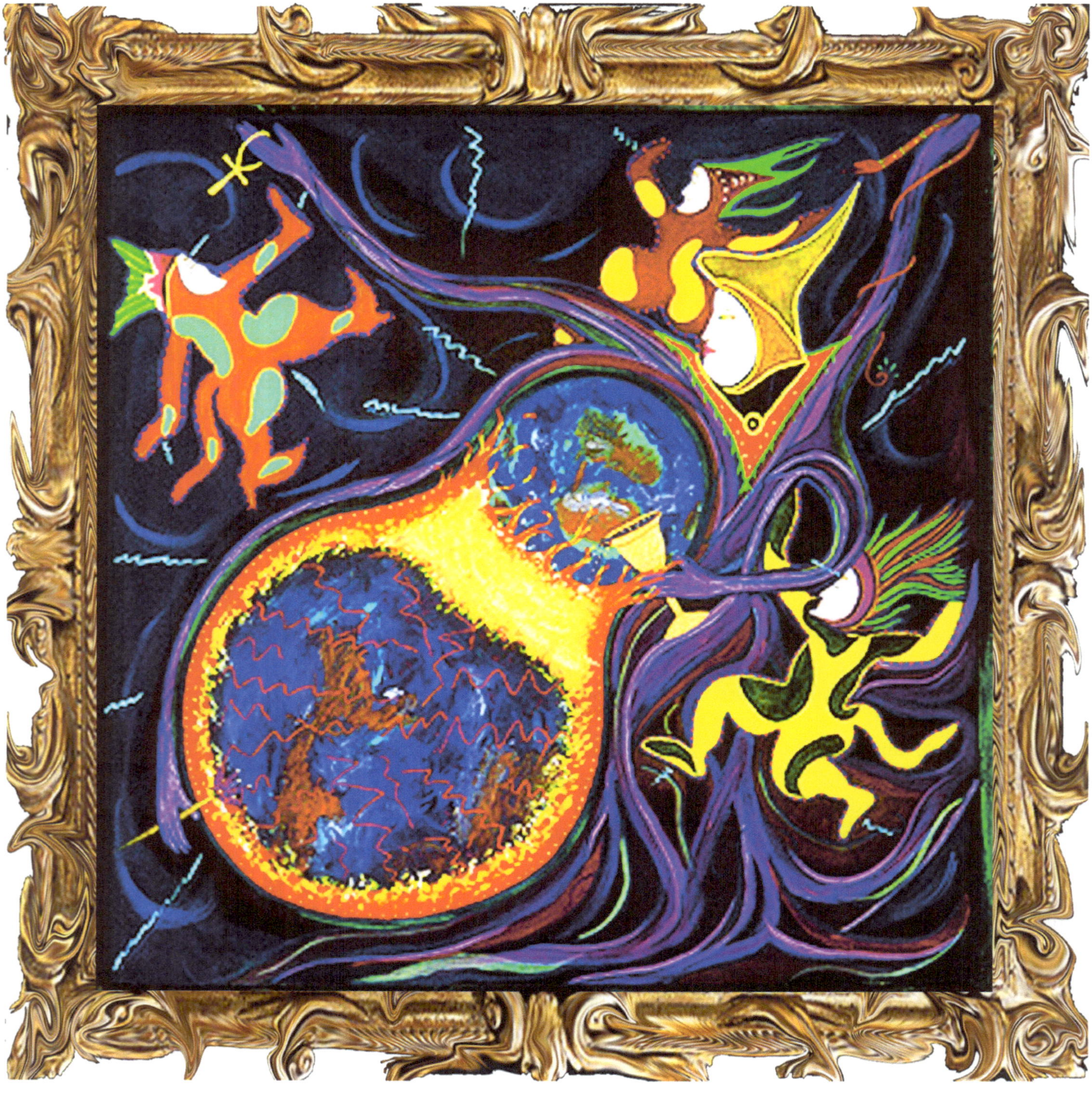

c. huilo c.

314

$\mathcal{C}$omplete darkness surrounded Lola. Three leonic beings marched forth from the void. Behind them rose a lovely guardian.

Crux Ansatata held several magical tools in each of her four arms. "Welcome Lola to the 9th Gate. Here, we invoke and bring forth a new Gaiaic realm of the physical form. We are surrounded by lovely Leonas who remind us of illustrious strength in beauty. Now, in order to generate a new Gaiaic realm, for this consciousness level, courage is necessary to transcend personal struggle. The humanos have experienced and shed so much pain and strife into order to grow. Now, along with this great serpiente upon my arm, we instill regeneration. Watch me a moment, will you?"

Lola observed the master as a large blue sphere appeared. It was the planeta of Gaia's. Crux poured a golden chalice over the stellar body. A gorgeous flower-topped wand was waved over the planeta. Finally, a bejeweled sacred Ankh was touched to the planeta's magnetica surface.

At once the planeta rumbled. Fire cracked through the surface and all the while Crux spun the globe faster and faster.

Crux decreed, "We invoke the *Law of Cycles. Law of Expansion. Law of Planetary Affinity. Law of Rebound.* These larger cycles of Gaia are now recognized as her humanos have reached their true essence. Harmonizing polarity, they have penetrated normal perception and risen to this place of sacred knowledge. I raise the lotus wand and call forth new beauty. All things happen in perfect time.

Unifying flames and water, we bring forth a new, blue lily of the sun. We invoke the 3rd ray with our leonas, known as the adapting factor. Adaptation is vital to a new dawn. Nothing shall bring down this life force on the planeta.

We marry 12 planetas to her and 12 points of the zodiacal intelligences. Rise up! Rise up! Rise up! New planeta, sacred eternal life. Pillars of duality joined in equilibrium. And so, it is done!"

Lola's heart beat so fast that their chest nearly exploded with joy. In front of them, Crux pulled forth a completely new planeta from the old one, which had now cracked and fallen apart.

"Here with the *Law of Planetary Affinity* and the *Law of Rebound* we simultaneously generate a new story bundle," stated Crux. "From the sinister and wild negativities, we summon a story that rebounds and grows more solid, sound and bold. This gate is the story of Faith in action!"

Lola observed the magnificence of the new planeta. Shimmering blue and full of wonder it was a place of new hope and possibility. Lola waved another roseheart key silently into the air and summoned Gate 10.

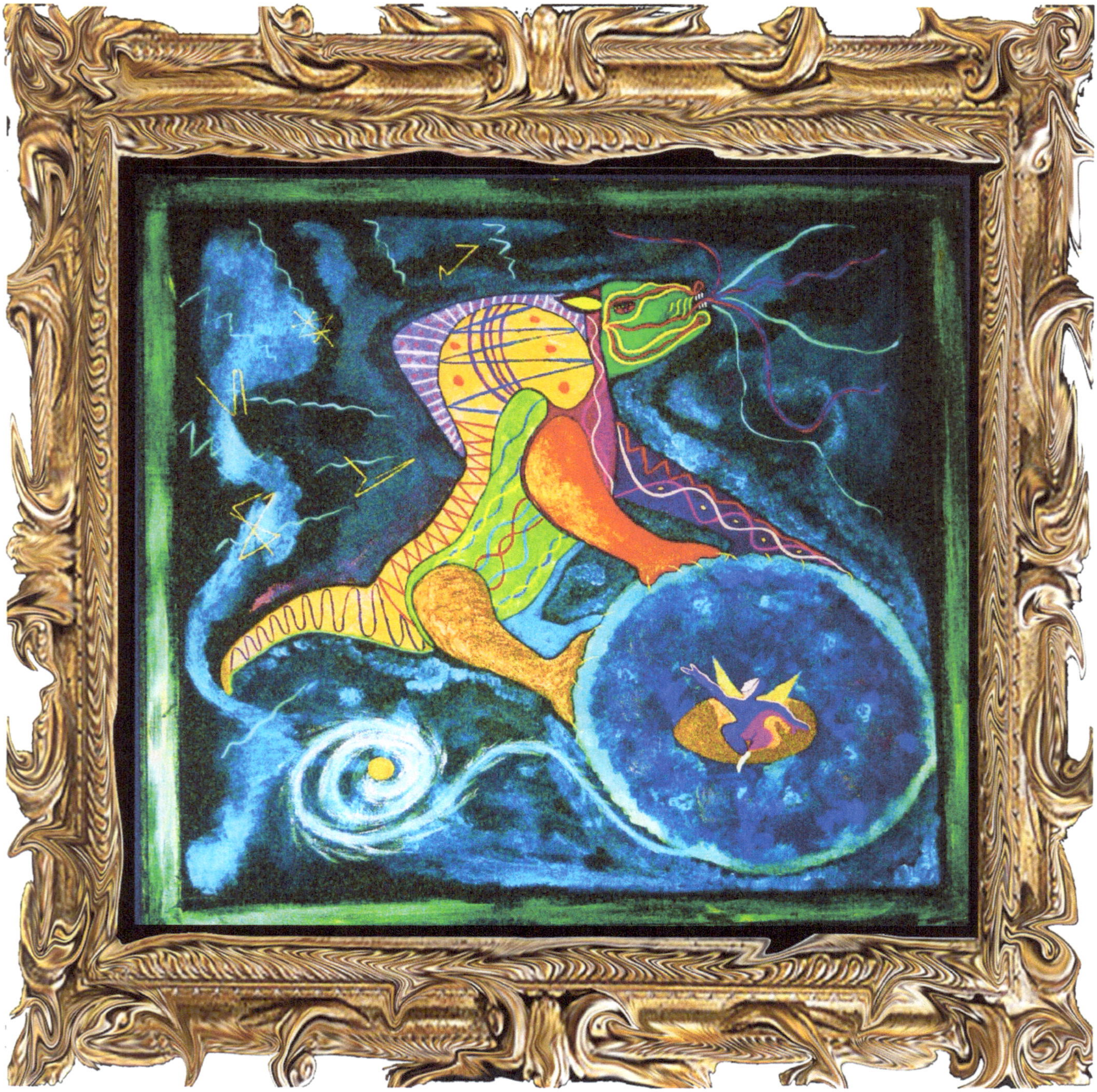

c. huilo c.

316

*T*he glowing new planeta slowly transformed itself into a spinning blue ball. Skeletals floated in the depths of its new liquid seas. Meanwhile, Lola rested in an animated state while observing wondrous things begin to form at Gate 10.

An enormous jaguar appeared with bright neon electrical grics surrounding its sleek body. Then with a flash of light, the new Gaia planeta with its skeletal heads bobbing in the new oceans began to twirl rapidly. The jaguar roared.

"I am Balam Nahuat," roared the mammoth Jaguar! "Listen to the great symphonies of the stars. The journey begins! Emerging out of fear into flourishing love. Out of desire to control into the desire to be present, I invite in and activate the synchronic matrix.

Let this resolve the errors humanos have made with false representation of sacred codes. I summon the return of this great energy, this majestic planeta to the deepest seat of knowledge. Hereby, there is no greed. No apathy. No jealousy. No entitlement. No complaisant manner. Here empathy has evolved into pure compassion. Lola, please join me in the great awakening of this gate!"

Lola stood in the dark space and raised their arms into the air. "I summon valor and fearlessness to boldly integrate consciousness with the unconsciousness."

Suddenly, in the distance a spiral of light formed. It swirled slowly and moved toward them. A green glow at its center began to get larger and shine brighter and brighter.

"Ah hah! Welcome Al Cy One," roared Balam. "Indeed, this is a vital connection—a renewed and new source of energy awaits the evolved Gaia. Now, I quicken these laws into actuality. *Law of Action. Law of Rebirth. Law of Cyclic Return. Law of Miracles. Law of Monadic Return. Law of Prophecy.*"

A voice rose from the giant emerald glowing star. Al Cy One resounded these declarations. "By acting. We Do. We Create. By rebirthing, we summon ancient obligations of the akashica accord. We awaken truths, ingrained qualities, solutions for revolting against injustices. We call forth the explanation of that which conditions humanos. We invite in what is said of them and to be truthful about who they actually are within the dynamics of the universal spectrum.

In this wheel of existence and possibility we summon from the incarnation of the third to the 5th dimension. There are 2 more gates of understanding and completion before this new essence is entirely birthed. All karma must be cleared and forgiven. Let the mastery of miracles be prevalent. Everything is a miracle and is acknowledged as thus. Through the sum of three influences of the Great Oso, the Seven Sisters and Sirius we bring these divine pilgrims into alignment with the prophecy. That foresight which many felt inside, is now generated into fullness through the universal telepathic field."

Balam spun the globe with sharp claws. Lightening bolted and illuminated the darkness. Balam spoke. "Let us bring forth the rebirth of innocence from the Kozmic egg. From all the past, present and future, and those yet to know, that with prediction comes supposition. When the All in the All and All in the All unfurl newness, the future is happening as just that… a manifestation of love. Energy changes from moment to moment and may this be set as the new *Law of One!* The tenth gateway is now open!" Lola raised one of the last 3 roseheart keys into the air. "Gate 11 here I come!"

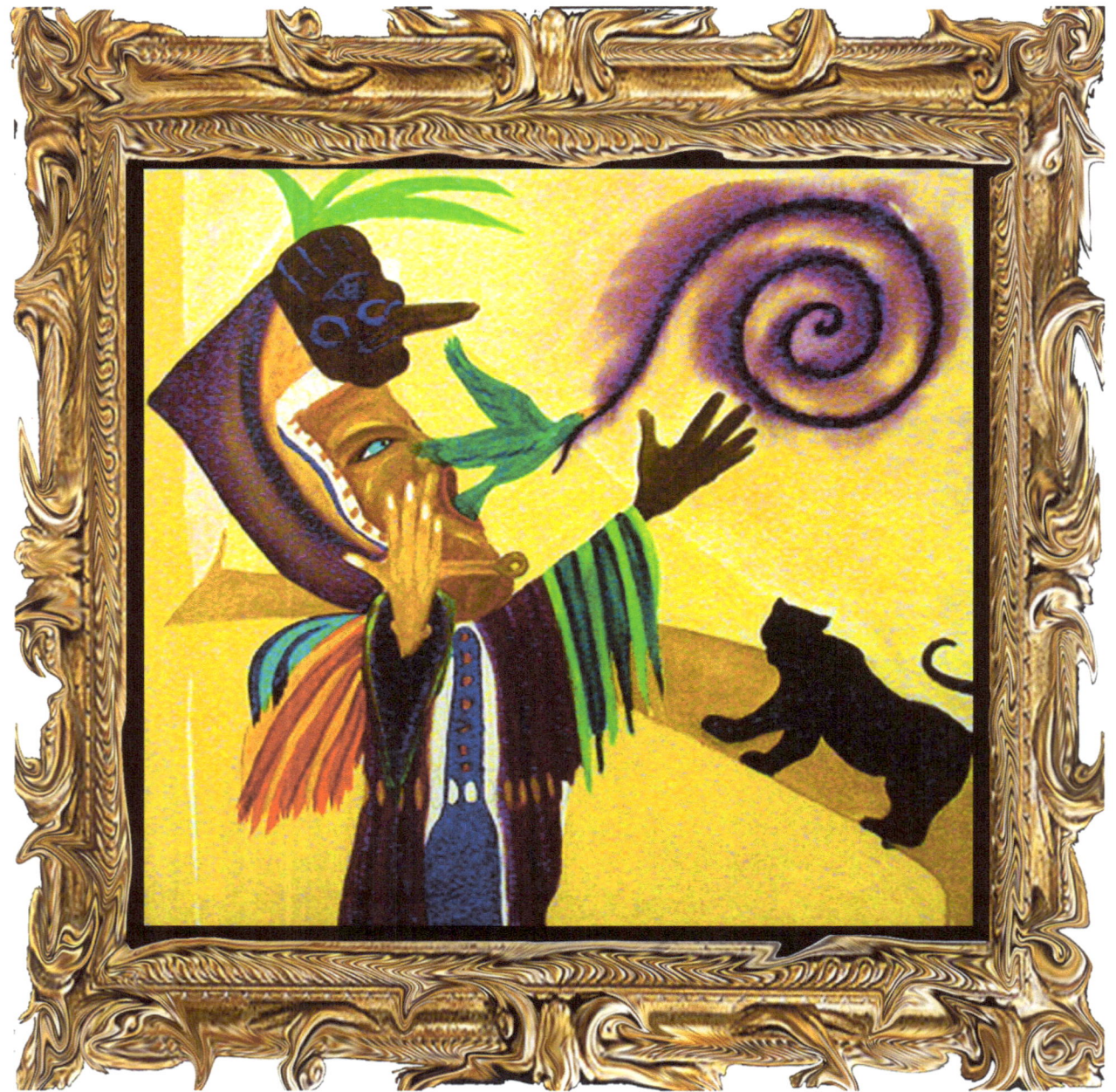

A soft electrical current surrounded Lola. The process of opening the gates of consciousness for the ascension codes was exhilarating. Each gate deepened the commitment, a level of integrity to participate along with the humanos and the entire miracle of the universe in order to expand and continue on its mysterious wonder.

Lola saw a faint light showing upon the horizon as if the sun was rising. Softly at first, heshe heard a lovely song. It sounded like the whistle or cooing of a bird.

"I summon the *Law of Grace*! The *Law of Abundance*! The *Law of Divine Flow*! The *Law of Faith*! The *Law of Forgiveness*! Come with me jaguar! Balam-coatl, for I am Coyopa, the Singer of Harmonies."

Instantly the light blazed brilliant, illuminating a wondrous being dressed in ornate feather plumage and indigo robes. As the reverent being sang, birds were birthed by each note from their mouth. They soared into the air, until there were so many they formed into a gigantic spiral in the air.

"Swansong was one of the lovely birds on my journey, who showed up at many of the magical circuses. Your song… if I may… is as lovely as that of the Phoenix," affirmed Lola.

Coyopa smiled. "The song I sing brings forth the spirit of Quetzal Coa tl. The great plumed serpent. The one who will descend to rescue the bone-seeds of humanity and bring them into union and reconciliation with the harmonic energy of the twin flame."

Lola moved closer to Coyopa. "The light here. It's so different. It's like, I can feel it."

"Indeed, you can. You are in the photon belt. This is the realm of celestial harmonics. Where one is merged with lightening and purified, thus completely transformed. Hence, igniting one's light body and rejoining with the ALL. Though never separate, this is where one abandons possession to the material worlds, engages spontaneity and the marriage of heaven and hells are formed."

Lola watched as a chocolate colored head emerged from Coyopa's crown. In the distance, Lola saw a large black leopard slowly approach them.

Balam-Coatl added to the chorus. "These laws. *Grace*. Where one is elegant, and eloquent at the same time. This is when one is completely aligned with the 'greater good of the ALL'.

Abundance. Here one has reached success. Surrendering oneself from the hoarding of material for that of sharing. The desired prosperity to gift each other with everything one needs in their heart's desires… though not necessarily that of material wealth. Here one engages in the gifts of love.

Divine Flow. Each one is committed to being of service—for the greater good of the ALL. Flowing at all times with the higher self, and creating actions that reflect love and allowing.

Faith. Here we find that one knows more than can be read, studied, heard or learned. One knows because they are part of the ALL. Faith is the direct link to universal wisdom.

Forgiveness. This is holiness. It is what holds the universe together. It is eternal virtue. Honorability is upheld when one maintains a state of non-violence. Quite simply… for giving more love.

Prayer. Concentrated focused will. A place of stillness and opening up. Indeed, Coyopa, your songs are requested for counsel with the ALL."

Balam-Coatl sat licking its paws for a moment. Lola waited calmly.

Coyopa cooed. "Balam-Coatl your words are divine! *Rhythm* is called upon. The breath of the divine feminina is blown with each lyrical tune, whilst with the same breath one inhales back the source. Everything flows. Death. Rebirth. New. Old. Reaching this gate, one has employed an active energy by manifestation of seeing truth as it really is.

And now, *Sound*. The plumed beings who soar between worlds and maneuver through the elements, their very songs, each song, invigorates a seed to sprout. Thus, is the *Law of Sound*. Every living thing has sound. The Universe is Sound. An enormous chorus. A divine symphony. Through our sounds, our songs, one has power to restore harmonic patterns. These are known as mantrams. Will you chant with me Lola and dear Balam-Coatl?" The three joined in a circle and sang:

Fare me a piacere?
Dive into a staccato!
Energize a fugue!
Spiral a rhythm for us
Chorus of symphonies
Do as you please
In the music of the spheres
For all the queers!

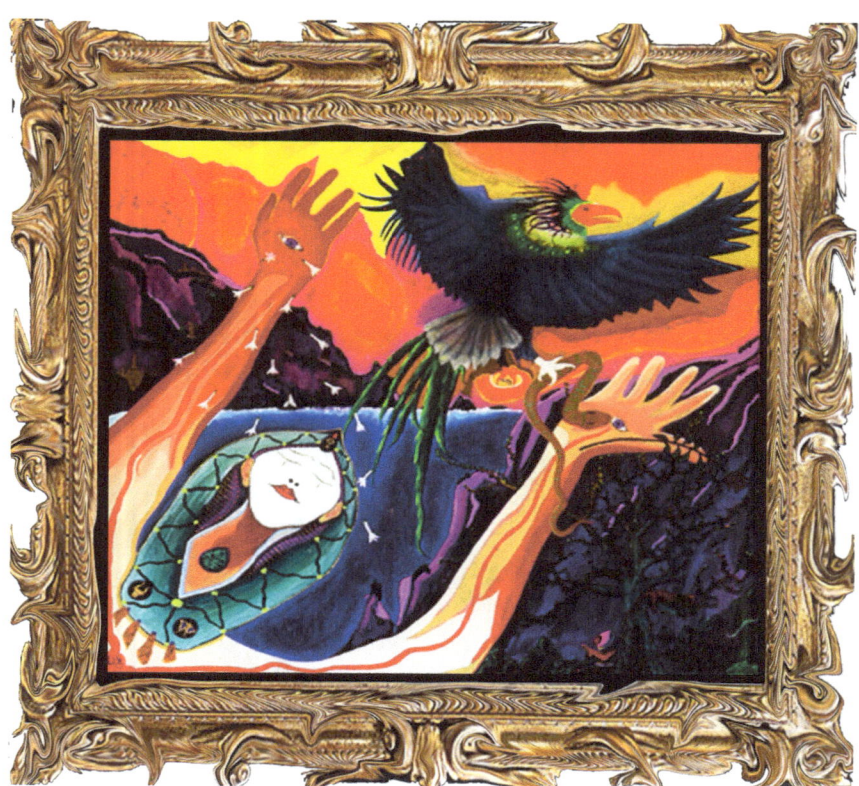

Lola wandered off into the sunset. Heshe sat in stillness. Immersed in the enchantment of the gates and their impeccable wisdom, Lola closed their eyes a moment. This quest was like no other.

"My desire is to mirror this incredible mastery, to reflect it in to everything and everyone I encounter." Lola heard water splashing on a distant shore. Swiftly, dazzling light filled the void so much so that Lola had to squint and shield their eyes.

Lola raised another rose into the air. "12th gate! 12th gate! 12th gate! I arise before thee, ready and willing. Reveal thy wisdome!"

A large-figure, who was extraordinarily dressed ran down a hillside to join Lola.

"I am Maha Yantra. Greetings. I bring forth the wonder of the Sri Yan Tra. The holy mystic wheel of life turning and turning… the presence of self forever ascending to know thyself. This shield contains 4 doors that lead to the 5th dimension."

Another being walked towards them from under a tree. The cloaked figure held a lantern and sat to join the other two.

"I am Hermastesis. The bringer of introspection. Here we illumine the final steps on the path to Euphoria. I have joined you from the depths of the underworlds—the dark night of the soul. And, now this light reveals the wisdom for all others to see… that all diversions may dissolve that may have prevented the union of higher with supreme self. At this gate we summon the Phoenix, the true aviary of regeneration. We hail the ouroborus and transmute any final doubt. We bring forth the new logos, the new word, the new glyphs of communication."

Lola took a deep breath. "My… my. I smell, …what a wonderful odor. Those flowers… they fall from the stars!"

"Yes! Jasmine snow. The final farewell to things no longer serving. A gift. A reminder of triumph over adversity. Confidence. Purification. Delicate yet resilient. Now, with each of you I bring forth the *Law of Balance. Law of Challenge. Law of Common Ground. Law of Disintegration. Laws of Healing and Law of Karma. Law of Order of Creation. Law of Process. Law of Radiation. Law of Sacrifice. And finally, Law of the Will of the Divine."*

Lola reached out and gathered the star-shaped jasmine petals and brought them to their nose. The aroma truly carried the scent of revolution.

"Indeed, balance creates stability from the turmoil of the 3rd dimension and integrates the equilibrium of divine wisdom," declared Hermastesis. "Challenges contain pertinent information required to change the qualities inherent in being 'ruled over'. Common ground guides one to problem solving and thus blend seeming differences into unified energy.

Disintegration… ah… yes… here comes the Phoenix to share," pointed Hermastesis.

The dazzling bird soared around the sky. "Shedding the sheaths of untruths. Discarding, devouring, melting with illusory death… only to bring forth the essence of immortality."

Meru Yantra joined the discussion. This glorious being had been sitting in a cave on the mountain. A divine teacher of faith. "Healing. Brain waves return to sync with the Gaia force. Removing obstacles, instilling sacred energy."

Lola stood up and walked over to a tree.

El Arbol shared their wisdom as well. "I am but one of many in my tribe. Arbol de Vida. Many of my kind live for thousands of years in one spot. We know the art of steadfastness and stillness, the passing of epochs. Karma. It is not referred to here as punishment, merely the understanding for causation.

What one vibrates with inside the mental planes is ultimately returned to the originator in some form. This is the operative that every wish leads to ultimate fulfilment. And thus it is so."

Phoenix swirled up again, clutching the ouroboros and serpiente, Transmuta. "In the Order of Creation, what is begun is carried all the way through to completion, that which was conceived in spirit has reached the level of a turning point."

"Lola have you something to offer of process, for yours has been a grande and a most admirable quest," shouted Hermastesis!

Lola reflected for a moment before speaking. "I feel this awareness. Process… is the wish, the heart's desire, to reach a certain goal… as was mine. I strived to liberate and awaken other jaguar magicians, the qweer beings, and their essential importance in the fabrik of society.

Humanos. and the energy of Gaia have moved into a new direction and thereby create harmonic order. I appreciate all that I have accomplished, and know that if I had skipped even one step, any of the difficult ones, I would never have arrived here as I am today." Lola bowed to the others.

Phoenix flapped its enormous wings and cawed. "Radiation and Sacrifice. The radiatory energy of humanos on the planeta of Gaia can no longer be confined to their mental prisons. The sphere has generated so much potent energy and is ready to expand to a realm of larger and wider expanse of conscious realization. It is there that there is also opportunity to transcend through each individual's self Sacrifice. The sinister and incongruent forms that prevented revealing the mysteries of life have dissolved. Now the 4th ray points to the 5th plane."

Meru Yantra tossed more jasmine petals into the air. "We are joined by the sacred holy mountain and the Kosmic Sea, the abyss from which all things come and depart. Here is the Will of the Divine. These gates assist in the development of a new world… freeing the divine soul to merge with unity of spirit. The 'crown' of consciousness, reaching the highest point… Though, currently there are even more sophisticated ones! For now, it is the Will for humanos to be divine. This will has pushed them forth into the new light. Lola take them to the 13th portal of ascension!" The Phoenix, swooped up everyone and flew into the golden dawn.

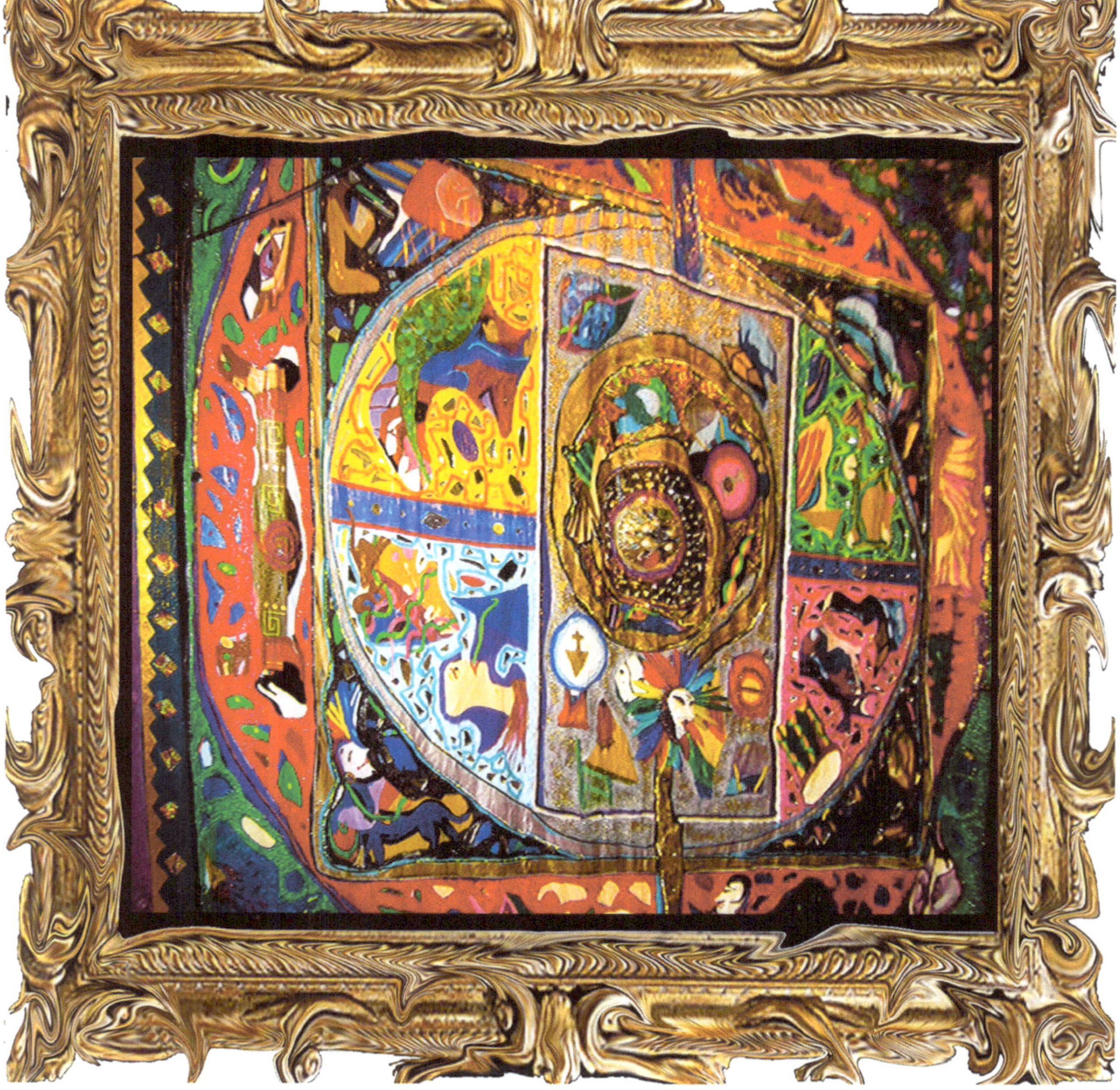

*L*ola waved the final roseheart key into the air. It was time. Traveling from gate to gate, from dimension to dimension, from the 'selva' to the urban jungles, Lola was ready for ascension or union.

It seemed a long time, a deep silence, nothing moved. Then… a brilliant golden disk began to spin and stationed itself a few feet in front of Lola. As the disk spun, images were generated from its center. Some shattered like mirrors. They formed a large geometric pattern, a mandala of healing. Several felinas appeared, Coyopa, Tellurusious, many others appeared. Lotus flowers bloomed. A giant tree grew to the side. A payaso formed below the spinning disk. In a way, it was as if all the other gates had merged into one. Perhaps there was only one gate, one level, mused Lola.

There was Hey Okey laughing in a corner. "You have arrived to a place you never left. Trickster be. Here we anchor, tether the light to the Gaiac field, and to the pineal 3rd eye of all beings.

This portal 13 is the stargate entrance. It awakens the starseeds and connects them to the stories of their divine lineage. You have reached the wormhole leading to the unveiling of all knowledge, the truth of the ALL of the All.

Here, each atom, their molten force, where all elements exist, the root. This is where the core is in a state of Oneness. Here all senses are joined. Time and space are resolved.

This is the place where there is creation of the actual oversoul essence. The source here is Elohim and of the Divine Twin Flame. The Nagual contains all dimensions in its consciousness. You are at 0-point. The Sea of Potential is before you where the unmanifest sits inside the ALLness." Lola observed the gigantic mandala as it kept shifting its imagery. Then, unexpectedly the voices of all the felinas spoke in unison, a sort of choir, yet not singing more like purring.

"This is the soul matrix, Lola. Here, sound ripples, rays of light animate the lower dimensions and invoke a prismatic essence consciousness—the divine mind. You are a universal dreamer, that is how you arrived. You are in alignment with the pillar of light of the higher self. As a transducer, you can emit the signal from this field of consciousness to others. This realm holds no duality. It is beyond tangible or even definable.

Here is the realm of soul birth, the return to source. One becomes aware of all the planetary energies that make up 'you' as consciousness."

Lola breathed in and exhaled slowly and deeply. Heshe wanted to enthrall in each phrase and be ever present with them.

The grande image before Lola, had four Phoenixes, one in each corner. They flew around the golden disk and each picked up a piece of shattered mirror. "We invoke the Laws of: *Gender. Ascension. Divine Love. Free Will. Good Will. High Will. Love. Non-Attachment. Present Moment. Rebound. Solar Union. Spiritual Awakening. Will Power.* These Laws are sacred to the universe. Through them we open all to higher frequencies of light. Let us review each of them.

Ascension is the process of losing one's separation from its divine-self. From here one no longer needs to leave the incarnational personality from Gaia to a live a finer existence.

Divine Love, as you have done, and so will many others like you, the jaguar magicians and more, have completed a round of reincarnation and developed such soul growth so that your vibrational speed enables you to merge with the divine. Not that you were ever separate, but to remember this is so.

The Wills. Thoughts are things that bind each other together to create circumstance. Yours, and others who reach here have used Free Will for soul growth rather than to lessen or stall soul growth. This Will is reached when one surrenders the ego, and here one can hang up their Soul-Overcoat of lifetimes."

Lola turned to the right and saw a lovely womun approaching and at her side was SwanSong.

"I am Sirrah of the body immortal. Lola, you have seen so many suffer in the realm of 3-D Gaia who have adversely affected Free Will. Let me speak to you about Good Will. This *Will-to-Good* is growing rapidly on Gaia. It presents more hope and assurance in solving problems, and each time it is integrated, the 'ill-will' gradually disappears.

Now, we speak of Love. Love is a commitment to the finest expression of Divinity. Love brings the best in relation to oneness. Love is an offering of forgiveness. Love is treating the other as the divine being of which it is—a manifestation of the ALL."

The jaguars spoke again. "Non-Attachment dissolves karma. It reminds one that the ultimate nature of self is empty. It creates present-ness. Indeed, through the practice of non-attachment, one realizes that time does not exist, thus invoking the *Law of Present Moment*. There can be no anxiety when one chooses to live in the present.

Lola, we wish to speak to you about the *Law of Rebound*. You have witnessed the dire state of the entropic chaos that has infiltrated Gaia. Such realms have in their codex when such negative energy fields are out of balance, to leap out of it, stronger, and bolder with more soul growth for all. This is a time where one observes a 'leap of faith'.

Do you see this sphere at the center, it is a solar disk. It holds the story of the *Law of Solar Union*. This integrates realms back to a natural pulse. It signals the opening of a hologram. Here is the I Am, We are, You are One. The light filaments here ae liquid plasma and enables one to be everywhere at once, all dimensions at once, time travel. This is the vortex of healing. This 13th portal is more than a representation, it is an activation. The *Law of Spiritual Awakening* has reached such a vibration where the light is clear. This is the place of the Diamond Light Matrix. It is a wormhole where one can see what is happening in the spiritual worlds. Here one is fearless and harmless. Certainly, a level of self-control and stability is required to maintain a vibration for awakening to this state of consciousness and many others beyond it.

Through this gate is brought forth higher forms of perception and power, it demands moral impeccability—its misuse can bring a fallen angel, hence grave karmic consequences. Now, let us call for the *Law of the Will of the ALL, God, Divine*."

There was a long moment of silence, a stillness, a sense of ALLness in a deep field of nothingness. The ALL is not questionable. The form-building of the ALL is within this law and no laws. Humanos must be divine and therefore, starseeds such as yourself, Lola, and many others after and before you, push creation towards divine light… the good. When one has reached towards greater harmony and realized through the power of balanced reasoning, one comes to trust in the good of all things in existence."

Lola felt heshe's body vibrating and pulsing so rapidly that they took flight. Once again, it was time for the flight of the jaguar magicians.

Hey Okey chuckled and pointed to small birds in the tree. "Lola look! The Flower Kissers have a message for you to take to your lovely kin, the androgynenes, epicenes, double-spirits, queer, gay…beings. And now and as it always has been… it is so! 13 gates of consciousness are now integrated into your divine beingness. Well done Lola!"

A vast space, like the inside of a cloud surrounded Lola. Pearly, sapphire light had replaced the giant mandala of the 13th Gate. It was iridescent and fluid-like. It was like being in a soft ocean of light.

Lola was calm. Heshe felt nourished, rested, but most of all strangely and wonderfully whole and complete. Gently, there was a sound of humming, a buzzing like bees, yet subtly different. It was the Flower Kissers and their cousins, the Flower Eagles. "Welcome great messengers from the Golden Realm! Indeed, I am joyful to be in the midst of your kin-dom of tranquility and harmony again. I wonder of news you may have of Gaia, the Planet of Great Consciousness."

As heshe said this, three jaguar magicians popped out of the liquid light and joined the group.

Jaguar Magian 1, Lamb Duh, spoke first. "It's as if many of the Magicians, dear Lola, have emerged from a state or Torpor, and a new enthusiasm is rising. What serendipity to follow you through the 13 gates!"

"You were with me? How cool. What strength and tenacity, the stamina to witness awakening with such courage and determination," exclaimed Lola!

Jaguar Magian 2, Effur Vez Scent, giggled. "We savored each moment as the flower kissers accompanied us on many levels. I feel tireless, a new sense of freedome. What a ceremony of wholeness!"

Flower eagles tittered. "Teee heeee teeee heee… life changing indeed. Restoration of sensibility. Adaptable and wise you are!"

The last of the blue magicians, Jaguar Magian 3, Unifica, spoke. "Life is an illusion, is it not? And with these gates, magical flashes of the divine! Our endurance of this journey we will share with others."

"Indeed. Here we all are, let's dance this joy. First, we reveal the messages. Now from heavenly realms, we bring laser light language to pierce the hearts that have turned to stone, those that were once seemingly unreachable.

We dose them with wild gratitude. Life is a process of enjoyment and not necessarily just the resolving of burdens. One becomes more agile when they learn to navigate circumstance and stay in sync with the divine rhythm. True, we have emerged from the Path of Great Beauty, and now a resurrection of possibility lives in each of our souls.

Now with this lightness of being, dance everyone! Dance! We must assertively seek out those that need our compassion and inspiration and renew them with their divine purpose, and bring forth the best in them."

One after another, Jaguar Magicians and their allies continued to jump out of the 13th portal. Hundreds, thousands, millions were remembering who they were and returning to oneness.

It seemed almost instantaneous. They spiraled the Planet of Great Consciousness into the 5th dimension. They flew into a new realm of time and space. No Fear. No Hostility. No guilt. No suffering or sense of separation. The mind unified. Gender was liberated. Mastery over attached thought. Universal energetic laws were in place. The free spirits flew into their new world and made merry with the faerie…

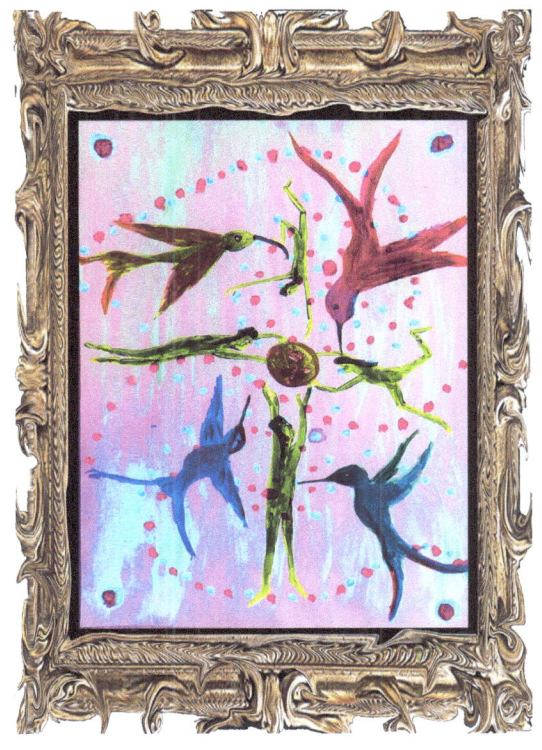

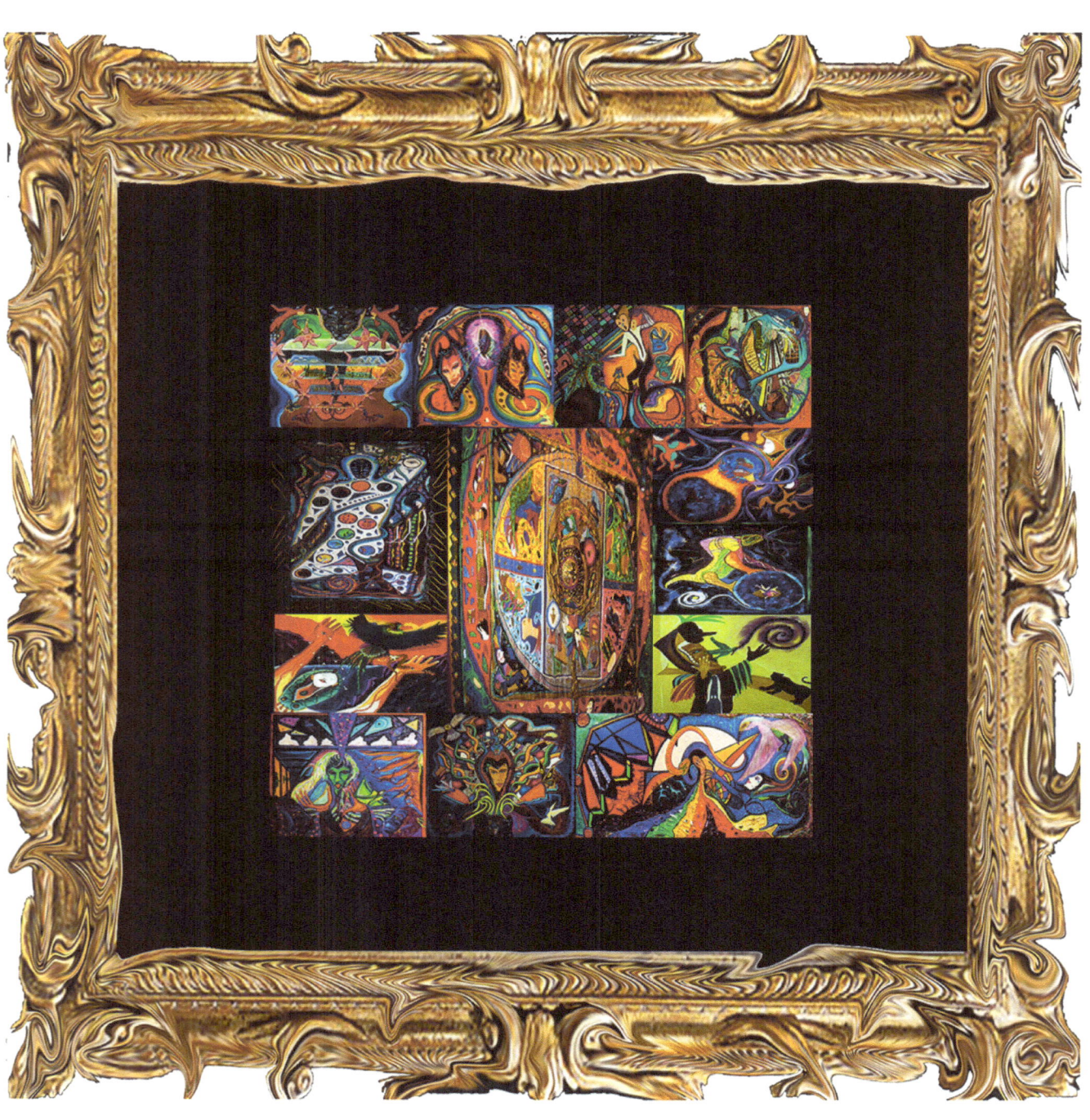

c. huilo c.

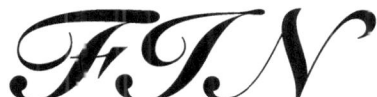

REFLECTIONS

After nearly thirteen years of painting, writing and theatrical vignettes, the complete *Tales of a Jaguar Magician* have arrived. What began as a singular dream in May, 2005 became a dream within a dream within a dream and so on...

Many times, I felt an affinity with masterful ancestors like the author and painter, William Blake or Frida Kohlo. Perhaps it takes centuries for an audience to understand and absorb the magic of one's writings or paintings. These writings may take hold in future generations as gender becomes more fluid and sacred inclusion of queer people reform society's ability to maintain equanimity.

The art, like many works before, whether sculpture, film or theatre often became my greatest teachers. As I became introduced to each character, I gave birth to a strange family. Each image became alive and shared its truth. It's a curious part of the relationship with art, when one engages the many selves from within and then reveal them to the external world. I enjoyed christening each character. Using whimsical rather than common names, each one referenced a particular aspect of their personality or position in the story. Symbolic as many are, the identity tags, (as I refer to them), would color the lyrical vibe of the narrative.

As I wrote each book, I realized it was a process to get to know myself through this specific art form. Writing is a complex skill, very different from the visual arts. It is a complete surrender to a hallucinatory world. Coaxing the story from my muse while gazing at the illustrations, each sequence jumped off the paper and danced onto the page. Some of the images began as simple sketches on a lazy afternoon at the beach, only later to be integrated into the unfolding story. For example, the image of Fractal Chick was nothing more than a frolicsome play on geometric patterns and the human form. Later, when I painted it, the colors pulled the character out and began to explain the possibilities of who they were and how they could further the tales.

Each book, though some more than others, required extensive research. Certainly, the last book, *Vibration of the Hummingbird*, took days exploring references on universal laws, dimensional qualities, ancient tomes and several more inquiries into what ascension could possibly offer to humanity during absolute chaotic times.

Eagle Eats Jaguar's Heart was especially interesting in how it was spawned. While on a layover in Mexico City at the airport, I gleaned through a tourist book on what to see near Villahermosa. I was mysteriously drawn to the ruins of Bonampak. The mystery deepened when I bumped into an old friend on my stay near the ruins of Palenque. I expressed to him that I had interest in seeing the temples of Bonampak and he delighted in my query. My friend picked up a jade sculpture in the formation of a sitting jaguar. One of its paws was outstretched and held a heart shaped piece of obsidian. "This is *you*," declared my friend! I studied the object wondering how it may be linked to more information about myself.

My friend shared a complex story of how there was a myth, *Eagle Eats Jaguar's Heart* presumed to be from a translated variation of ancient Mayan myths. He shared that the jaguar was incredibly passionate about the pleasures of the earthly realms. So much, so, that it was keeping the feline in a state of sorrow. One day Eagle came to release jaguar's heart by eating it, thus helping the jaguar to live more in the present and live without attachment.

Then, as my ally shared more details, he expressed how the temples of Bonampak had kiosks on the steps of a pyramid that had remains of various murals on their ceilings. In one of the kiosks were images that referred to this exact story.

The next day we set off to the temples which were still rather remote, hidden from vagrant tourism, in the Lacandonian Jungle near the Guatemala border. These temples were still barely uncovered from the vigorous jungle vegetation that had covered them for centuries. As I walked into one of the Kiosks and gazed up at the mural, I felt a deep affinity with these people. Later, I went to lie down on an old stone wall. While in a daze, I would shut my eyes and each time I opened them I saw either a hummingbird or butterfly hovering over my head. Magically it seemed, images of this tale wanted to be retold through my art. I had been brought to this mysterious site for a larger reason.

The books actually had many surprising mystical revelations, or *revealings* throughout the 13-year journey of manifesting the tales. Dreams, visitations, experiences, and exposés from friends, were all part of the unfurling tomes. As I began to dive into the profound aspects of the books, important interpretations of shadow emerged. Some of these images had quite disturbing origins.

For example, in Tome 1 there is the image of the *Top/Bottom* and *Versa* characters jumping out of the *Urn of Desire*. In fact, these images were developed to indicate my ambivalence about which sexual position one preferred, let alone the harmful tone it promoted with regards to a hypermasculine/patriarchal state of being. Sadly, those labels and segragation tactics which were common in the bar scene of the 70/80/90's, etc. are still common in current social media formats.

In Tome 2, Lola cuts through the doubt matrix. In fact, I sketched this image to express my anger during the night I broke up with a boyfriend in Mexico. So, in fact, some of these images were relevant, at first, to passages in my own life as a gay man.

Throughout Tome 4 there are a few images that were generated from frightening or creepy experiences. For example, a boyfriend who had gone berserk towards me in Costa Rica, became the image of Lola getting punched through the heart by their divine twin.

The shadow references with *Delusionata* and *Ambivillota* in the book actually refer to an extremely weird experience I had in the mountains near Bolzano, Italy. I was staying at a friend's house, when one night, a bed lamp kept turning itself on, even though I turned it off over and over. Thinking it was an electrical short, I let the event go and went back to sleep. However, the next night was even more spooky. I had unplugged the light. When I woke up suddenly around midnight, the light had been mysteriously plugged back into the socket and illuminated. I turned if off, alarmed and unnerved. Then, later that night, I felt a pressure, as if someone was sitting on my bed. I woke up, alarmed and gazed into the far reaches of the attic on the opposite of where I slept. In the shadow, I saw the hint of small child, eerily standing in a corner. At this time, I turned the light back on and kept it on for the remainder of the night. The next day I burnt some sage and smudged the room. I also did a tarot reading to see if spirits wanted to speak with me.

The series of paintings which became the ascension portals, began as a way for me to teach myself about the prospects of entering or seeing my way into the fifth dimension. I had done several plant medicine ceremonies that revealed greater sensitivity for me to experience other worlds beyond the finite mundane. Hence, I decided through guided imagery and stories maybe I could assist anyone who was interested to invite in possibilities of other dimensions. Perhaps they could do this without having to engage in concentrated plant journeys or other focused new-agey programs.

With my background in the advertising arts, I understood how potent images could be with regards to shifting perception and most certainly, desires. Cones and rods in the eyeball quiver when specific colors are placed next to each other, like cerulean blue and crimson red. These also enhance the illusory vision of 3-D imaging. I began to couple this with the possibility that maybe, if I used intense, saturated color palates, dynamic geometric shapes and metaphor, perhaps I could stimulate the pineal gland to release DMT and activate, or unlock, strands of DNA linked to the 'god-code'.

This brings up several topics at once that may be approached better in a separate document.

However, in some schools of thought it is believe the chemical Dimethyltryptamine (DMT), could invigorate an undeniable relationship with the self and the soul, and the god-like or munificent self. Curiously one evening, while attending a soiree in Sonoma County, California, I shared my theory of art and activation of the pineal gland with a M.D. She listened intensely and expressed that there was certainly a realistic possibility to the idea. She explained that there were many inherent connections between the eye tissue and the pineal gland. Therefore, she deducted that perhaps there was sizzle in my approach that by painting specific imagery one could stimulate the eye and thus the pineal gland.

Whether this was true or not, I began to create what I referred to as the Jaguar Portal paintings in small studio in Puerto Vallarta around 2007. However, it's important to note that one of the first paintings was actually germinated while staying at a remote artist sanctuary in New Mexico. It is referred to as the electric jaguar. I sought to make the paintings as one would conjure a Bodhisattva. The viewer could meditate on the image and become 'one' with it and thus build mental bridges to transcend dimensions. The paintings, now the illustrations for much of Tome 5, were devoted to assisting neural coding, or the 'idea' of seeing one's way into the 5-D world of 'one-love'.

In the final book, the image of the 12th gate where the phoenix is released from Maha Yantra into the golden dawn, this painting was actually birthed by sketching a silhouette of my torso. Originally, I had painted this image as part of wooing a boy whom I never met. Ah, unrequited love turned into a valuable piece of art!

Wildly, several of the paintings were severely damaged and some even caught fire. One night, after an eclipse of the moon, or the 'blood moon', in 2007 several paintings of mine were slashed to pieces by a manic person. While preparing the paintings for departure to Mexico, I had left them in a studio space at an artist sanctuary in New Mexico. Early that morning, I set off from the land with friends to get groceries and perform other tasks.

The universe has its way to alarm us to upcoming situations, if only we would listen to our intuition. On the way driving out on snow covered roads, my truck sank and nearly toppled onto its side submerged in 4 feet of slushy water. I felt the sense it was time to turn back, however my friends inside the car were desperate to get out as they had been snowed in for a couple of weeks. Thus, against my intuition, I rallied and we continued onward and the car was towed out of the mud.

Later that night, upon return to the sanctuary, I went immediately to sleep. However, the other residents on the land heard screaming and shouts of *"I want to off Huilo!"* They ran down to the commotion and found the crazed man shaking in front of a pile of my artwork. The entire collection of jaguar portal paintings had been shredded or violently tossed onto the gravel road. The next morning after I wandered through the tears from sobbing residents, I approached the paintings wondering what had caused such a burst of violence to my artworks by someone whom I had never known.

That prior month, I visited an infamous community in northern Italy, known as Damanhur and their amazing Temples of Humankind. During the visit, the administrators invited us to explore synchronicity and be mindful of those that shared the 'tour' with us, they may be intrinsically part of our life's journey. Subsequently, I met a psychic from Malibu who became pivotal in the unraveling of several malicious events that damaged or destroyed several paintings in the years to come.

I phoned my new friend in Malibu after the incident in New Mexico. I queried her magical skills to see if she had any clues as to why the images may have been the target of such ferocious behavior. She expressed that it sounded like an entity attack, something along the levels of the inorganic beings referred to in Carlos Castanada's work, The Dream Awakening. Evidently for some reason, these energy beings often sought out vulnerable humans and directed them to perform malicious behaviors in order to upend evolutionary growth of human consciousness. Hence, the nearly total destruction of the first rendering of the Jaguar Portal paintings continued to be prey for malevolent forms. It seemed whomever they were, for some reason, seemed to target my devoted attempt to liberate humans from 3-D fixed realms. After surveying the shredded paintings I decided to create, what I refer to now as, the 13th Gate of Consciousness.

In 2009, I went on an artist sabbatical in Spain. I traveled with the mindset of painting 13 ascending gates of consciousness. I chose to use a format of painting transparent screens. This used a technique of creating images with watered down acrylics onto see-thru fabric. Later in the residency, I engaged them for an installation work and directed experimental video through the 'screens'. I also employed storytelling with masks while dancing through the room. While painting the images, I could not 'see' the 13th portal and decided in its place to leave the final gate as an empty space or a completely white canvas to symbolize an unformed gateway.

Consequently, after the paintings received a bashing at the retreat in New Mexico, I began to visualize and thus manifest the 13th portal. I took the shreds to Mexico and with a former lover created a substantially large mural. The piece was exhibited at Gay Pride in San Francisco and then later at various shows. The final presentation culminated at the Symbiosis Festival next to Pyramid Lake, Nevada during the annular eclipse of 2012. I placed the painting on the desert ground and surrounded it with 12 transparent screens which had been created years before Spain.

It seemed like a wild, yet incomplete story. Therefore, I transferred the mural to its final resting place in Costa Rica in 2014. I hung it on the ceiling, like the renderings at Michelangelo's Sistine Chapel.

In 2010, while working on the manuscripts for Tomes 2 and 3, I placed photographs of the illustrations on the wall of a cabin I had rented with a lover in the southern Andes of Chile. One morning, I descended to the first floor of the house and saw plumes of smoke coming between the boards of the wooden walls. I realized the house was on fire. Once the flames were put out, I saw that the second story had nearly completely burnt. I went upstairs and found shriveled photographs from the illustrations on the charred floor. Once again, it seemed something had attempted to drive the message to terminate the story that I was working on. It was like it some mysterious effort was attempting to thwart my quest to liberate humanity from the 3-D realm via Lola and queer magical consciousness.

The dramatic event turned my direction once again towards Costa Rica, land of the jaguars. I returned and began, with the help of locals, to build a wizarding school of consciousness and residential arts center in the southern mountains near the border of Panama. One day in 2013, I finished the last paintings for Tome 3. The lovely painting of Circo Duende with Loquatia hung in my studio. I went upstairs to the second floor and suddenly received an alarming instinctive voice that said, "Your painting is on fire!" I ran down the steps and found the illustration in flames. I quickly pulled it off the wall and put out the fire. The flames had burnt the left corner of the painting, but luckily most of the major elements of the image were unharmed. Once again, strange events sought to destroy illustrations from the books.

By studying the potential of the painting, rather than destroy it, I decided to enhance it. I had studied book arts in San Francisco a decade earlier and thought I could 'dimensionalize' the image by adding pop-out techniques to the picture. Meanwhile, I wondered in the back of my mind what was going on with my art and the frequent, crazy destructive energies that homed in on the Tales of a Jaguar Magician.

A year or two later, I received elder guests who were integrated into the circle of grandmothers. The women were part of a women's counsel who summoned each other to speak of ways to promote Earth's recovery. One of them explained to me the compelling story that Costa Rica was known in some circles as the 'crossroads of the tribes'. She explained further that it was also determined to be the critical 'jaguar bridge' that would connect the eagle and the condor.

The story of the eagle and the condor was gleaned from the Amazonian myth that speaks about the separation of human society onto two paths. I expressed to the elder that it was my intention with the Center to integrate the spiritual relevance of the jaguar story by reacquainting visitors to the 'subtle energies' and healing through the arts. At some point on my journey I had read that the jaguar also represented a mythological metaphor eluding to the jaguar gods transporting the arts up from the underworld, and thus turning the sun into gold.

The tension continued up to the present day surrounding the images for the books. In 2017, a former lover, set fire to the main building at the campus in Southern Costa Rica. Inside were several magical works, including the 13th portal, the white wizard sculpture (a.k.a, balam—the jaguar god), Esmeralda the Jungle Sorcerer as well as an original transparent screen that illumined an image from Tome 1. It depicted Lolaboy deep in the magnificence of the jungle, which also signified their innocence. Suspicious that once again the works, and now even an entire Center, were the focus of an inorganic being's mayhem.

I sought out clues to what may have been behind the veil of such horrific violence to beauty. While doing the final residency to create the last two manuscripts for Tomes 4 and 5, I became acquainted with an intriguing blend of quantum physics, DNA and astrology. The amazing astrologer reviewed my astral chart for my former lover who had perpetrated alarming events. The tragedy nearly destroyed the potential for the art and ecology mystic's outpost. The astrologer mentioned that his star-chart revealed the fated possibility that this scourge was at the hands of Draco walk-in. While the mundane may refer to the association of draconian as being stern laws from ancient Athens, some believe it is another form of intergalactic reptilian-like being. To those that believe we come from the stars, perhaps, beings come here to transmute ancient karmas. Whoever they are, or if this was the case, there may be an infinite number of possible races that prefer to have the human race modified and controlled.

To some, the idea that the veil between worlds on Earth has been populated by several other energy beings, is a farce. However, based upon the link between catastrophic events, it certainly had me wondering that perhaps something beyond the mundane was involved. With the books in their final rendering, I felt compelled to share the deep mystery behind the creation of their story.

As I write this, I remember one other, seemingly indescribable event. While performing a series of vignettes from the books, I portrayed the character, *Ametist Mal O Kyte Rutilated Quartzessa, Keeper of the Realm of Gems and Jewels* at a Hollywood theatre. As I moved a large marionette up and down on pulleys, I recited an incantation from the book with regards to the aforementioned character. During the scene I had, what I refer to as, a spontaneous time travel event. I energetically, mysteriously left the stage for a few moments and came back. I was completely unsure of where I had gone or what had happened. I quickly checked to see if the audience had noticed my swift change of behavior and none was noted. Later, while back at my residence, I reviewed the video sequence recorded during the astral travel event. Astonishingly, the video had stopped exactly at the moment I had the ethereal incident! Interestingly, one of my intentions during the Hollywood performances was to liberate, or purge demonic energies that the film industry was setting lose on viewers through the casting of sinister elementals.

Over the years, it became clear that there were inexplicable forces which for one reason or another did not want magicians messing with the status quo. Releasing control upon the collective human conscious and liberating it from the fixed, dominate power of the 3-D realm was apparently interesting to more than just me.

Whether anything is true or relevant can be debated, but the artist who creates from a deeply mystical source often has much to contend with that the reader may never come to know. Thus, it's why I write this final missive after over a decade of work on a deeply devoted story about the critical timing for unification of the dual state consciousness before the Earth is destroyed.

However, this subject is also up for investigation. As I stated in the forward of this series, I often wondered why were queer, gender fluid people such a threat to society? I mean, really, in a dangerously over-populated world, one might consider the need for a species to produce gender-neutral beings to offset spawning (like deer). Science aside however, rather than over-simplify the possibility of essential aspects for a species to generate same-sex loving beings—not just for suspending breeding consequences but maybe we exist for our lambda/unifying gender consciousness capabilities and to thwart aggression.

Hence, I want to explore briefly the background of the mythos regarding the joining of the hero twins. There are many myths that speak of the separation or reunion of twins, and this certainly is symbolized in the tomes with the integration of Lolaboy and their divine twin, Morgano. Metaphorically this is also a way to study the perspective for a state of what I refer to as, lambda unfied consciousness. The lambda super-consciousness is associated with a very high frequency brainwave (vibration of the hummingbird), wholeness (gender binary resolution) and integration (queer consciousness).

While I do not proclaim to be a behavioral or social scientist, I do have an innate ability to sense things. Certainly, there is much to be revealed in the relationship of cross-over gender variant behaviors and the evolution towards whole-brain thinking. Could it be, especially in a patriarchal world, that queer-minds might pose a threat to the fall of masculine control-dominated behaviors on Earth? Perhaps by examining the prolonged perception of self in gay-identified males may reveal minute changes to the evolutionary process of bridging neural fibers between the hemispheres of the brains, and thus whole-brain thinking is increased. The two sides of the brain have long been linked to female or male qualities. I wonder, that by upsetting the binary male paradigm to lean more towards the mastery of the compassionate male, whether same-sex loving or not, it brings to the table that queer consciousness could be a critical link in saving the human species from complete collapse.

Far-fetched? Maybe not. It has become increasingly clear that the machismo masculine dominating paradigm is showing signs of collapse. The new maleness, enhanced through queerness, is catalyzing shifts to a less violent, controlling masculinity, of which can surely be witnessed at times in many gay men. This is not to say transgendered, cis-gendered, lesbian and all the other possibilities of gender are not equally as important to the evolution of consciousness and the species.

Future generations will have to decide, sooner rather than later, and determine whether these tomes are useful in unraveling the depth of gender variations, their essential and integral contribution to a healthy society—rather than the current paradigm that being queer or gay is a threat to society and the meme of 'it gets better'.

Now, as I send these books off into the plethora of texts exploring mysticism and gender and the evolution of consciousness, I have also come to understand the importance of such works. Beyond egotistical attachment, I do feel that the more we tease new ideas into the world creatively on behavior changes and their linked effects on the well-being of the planet, I hope *Tales of a Jaguar Magician* will inspire audiences to think more creatively and beautifully about who we are, the very potential of the human being in the grander, mysterious cosmos.

As you turn the pages of this book, let the images linger in your limbic dreaming mind for a few moments. These images have been carefully mastered to clue your neural coding with pattern tracking elements and liberate who we are and how we feel about being human. New myths are always at risk, yet, I believe that humans thrive when we tell our stories creatively, not falsely, but imaginatively and innovatively. In turn, they help us to see ourselves in a new way for living in peace and harmony.

My dear reader, thank you for being a part of this journey. I have enjoyed every minute of the creation. The events have catalyzed me onward rather than pushed me down. I now step aside and will let Lola warm your hearts with this new mythos of queer, gender fluid beings as indispensible to the health and wellbeing of the ever-evolving human being.

Lastly, my advice to everyone is that, magic is real. Be ever so mindful with every word, written or spoken one increases the rate of conjuring or attracting events. Remember that magic is not necessarily some form of hocus pocus so much as it is the art of focused will. We create what we get with every thought. As we collaborate in the bridging of the new consciousness realms, remember you may get what you ask for, even quietly with yourself. Therefore, learn how to master your magic and direct intentional thinking for the greater good. We are in this together, jump in see who you are with, these are the ones you have been waiting for...

Into the light we go,

c. huilo c.

May, 2018

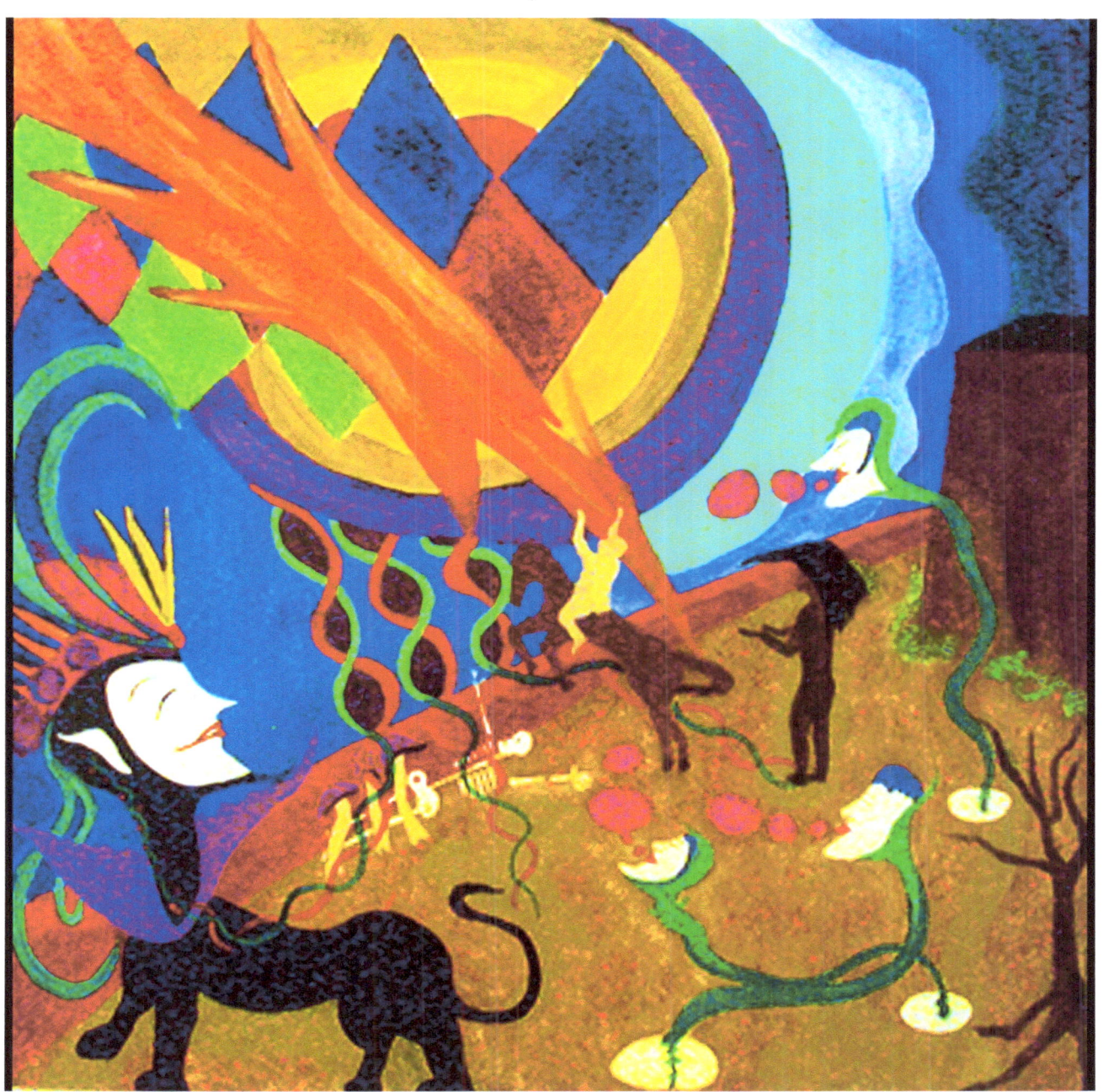

This is one of the images shredded in the desert.
It was literally Lola and Ocelotl jumping across the bridge from 3-D to 5-D.

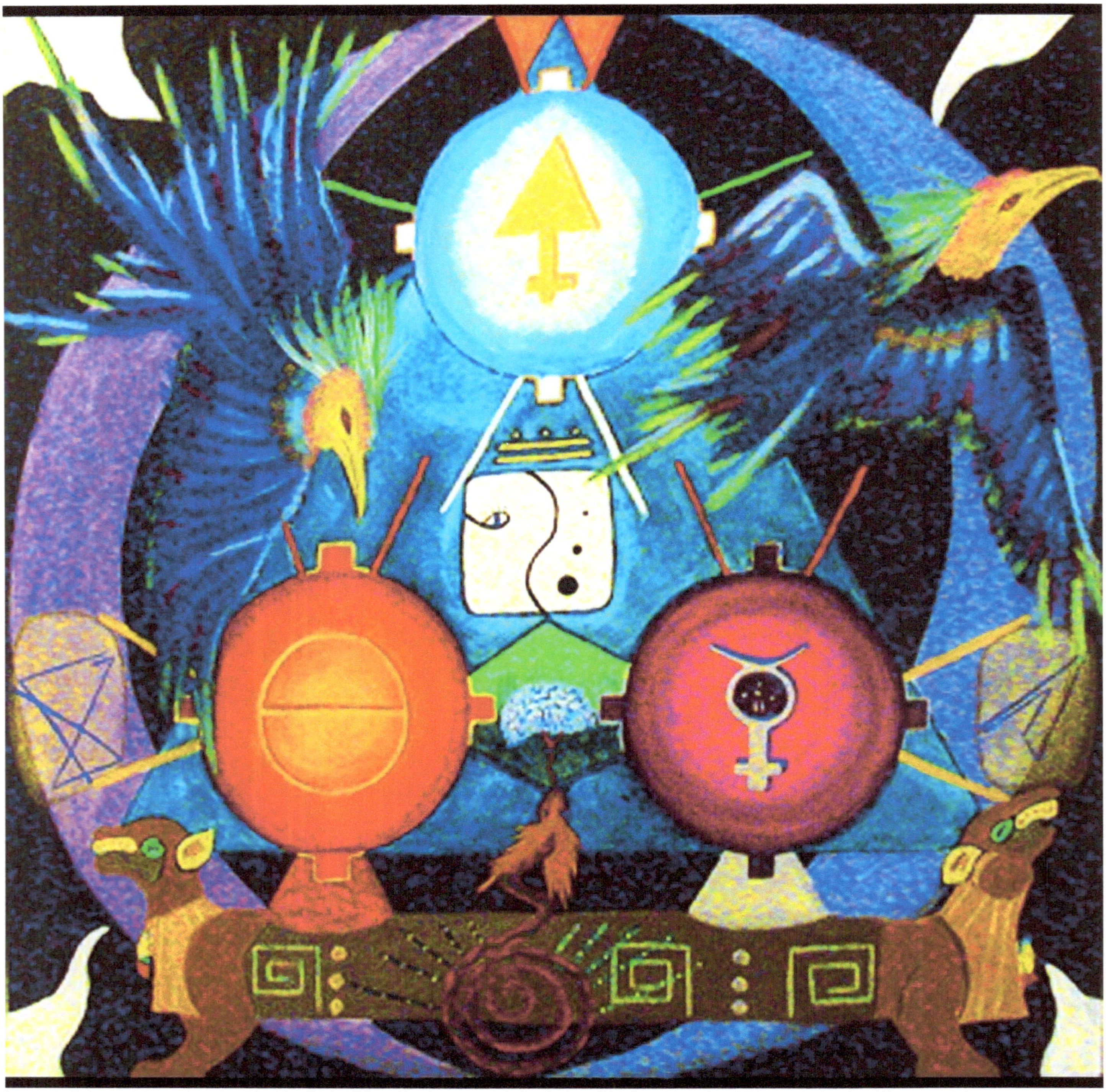

One more image of the several shredded at a desert sanctaury.
This one referred to the magic of sacred geometry and the story of alchemy and the jaguar magicians.